Praise for Messages from the Womb

"Claudia Raiken breaks new ground in the experience and understanding of pregnancy and birth. *Messages from the Womb* is all about listening—listening to oneself as a mother-to-be. Listening to the life growing in the womb. Listening to the throb and pulse of the universal truths surrounding the entire experience that emerge in our dreams and images. She brings to this book her unparalleled and extensive experience as a doula, as master practitioner of *DreamBirth*, and as leader of SOI's *DreamBirth* programs. With her inspiration as impetus, we co-created *DreamBirth* with expert doulas as a way to bring the power of dreaming and imagery to the birthing process. She now shares with you her own work and observations from the "womb." Her supportive and loving voice has helped many an anxious mother navigating conception, pregnancy and labor, finding through listening to the messages from within all that is needed to bring forth a new life. Take a look at what she says, test it for yourself. You will be forever grateful that you did."

—**Catherine Shainberg**, PhD, Founder/Executive Director of The School of Images (SOI) and author of *DreamBirth, Transforming the Journey of Childbirth through Imagery* (Sounds True, 2014).

"I highly recommend *Messages from the Womb* for families having their babies and for the professionals supporting them! The heart of the book is all about helping you and your baby communicate, and together learn how to transform issues arising to create the most optimal experiences—preconception forward. Claudia shares family stories that beautifully illustrate what she has learned from babies and their parents and how she has guided parents through the simple and brief meditative imagery exercises to tap not only their inner wisdom, but receive the wisdom of their baby. As you read the stories, your higher mind and heart wisdoms can awaken to expand your moving through your pregnancy, birth and bonding with more ease and joy. In the second half of the book, Claudia provides you with scripted exercises to help you and your baby address many of the specific situations that can arise during conception, pregnancy, and birth and bonding. This book opens new possibilities for conscious living with your baby from the very beginning of life. Quite a treasure."

—**Wendy Anne McCarty**, PhD RN, Author, *Welcoming Consciousness: Supporting Babies from the Beginning of Life*. www.luminousbaby.love

Messages from the Womb

Claudia Rosenhouse Raiken

Copyright © 2024 by Claudia Rosenhouse Raiken

Published by IML Publications LLC
www.imlpublications.com

Distributed worldwide by Ingram Content Group
www.ingramcontent.com

Book cover graphic design by Erin Rea
www.erinrea.com

Cover Artwork by Claudia Grotzek
www.claudiagrotzek.de

Interior design by Zhaoying ZHU

Interior layout by Medlar Publishing Solutions Pvt Ltd, India
www.medlar.in

Permission granted from Sounds True and Inner Traditions for the use of Dr. Catherine Shainberg's Visualizations.

Paperback ISBN: 978-1-955314-32-9

EPUB ISBN: 978-1-955314-33-6

Library of Congress Control Number: 2023948719

IML Publications LLC
151 First Avenue
New York City, NY 10003

"We are here to laugh, to play. It's something the mother can still have, even if the answer is, 'No,' or 'Not yet,' or, 'Never,' or, 'Love me later.' We are always around, and it would be good to be listened to more. We are here to make your life better, less lonely. More loved."
—from a baby soul.

Imagery as it is done in this work is the way to move the inside and the outside!

"Imagery is the language of the Universe."
—from a baby soul who teaches.

Babies Talk

Messages from the Womb

Through Guided Visualizations

Expanding Our Hearts and Minds

Claudia Rosenhouse Raiken

Dedication

With more love and gratitude than I can truly express, I dedicate this book to:

Blanche Evan, Pioneer Dance Therapist, who recognized in me, in my early 20's, great creativity and wisdom. I could feel you cheering me on, Blanche. Thank you, it helped more than you know.

Patricia Masters, renowned Psychic and friend. Patricia, you taught me how to look inside, and be in awe of that which truly supports us. You taught me the concept of first connecting with the divine, and then with my clients and students. I still feel you around me. I am forever grateful and miss you so very much.

Catherine Shainberg, PhD, teacher and mentor, world expert in *Saphire®* Imagery and Dreams, creator of *DreamBirth®* Imagery, you opened up this world to me, and gave me my true passion and vocation. I continue to learn from you, awed by your creativity, knowledge and insight. There are no words in the English language to thank you enough for how you have enriched and transformed my life. May our lives continue to intertwine!

Julianna Forgione, psychic and channeler of "The Group," you came into my life at the time this book was being conceived. You amplified my ability to hear my soul and taught me tools to manifest, that which could be. You have been instrumental in the growth of my confidence and in understanding that the book needed to be birthed. As you put it, it has a life of its own. Your enthusiastic first read of the manuscript clinched the deal!

To my incredible daughters, Iris and Amber, and my husband Larry. My life would not be as rich and full as it is without the three of you. It would, in effect, not be my life. Thank you, thank you for your love and support. I love you back with all my heart, and am more and more proud, Iris and Amber, of who you are becoming. Patricia Masters saw, many years ago, that you would become balanced and loving, as well as successful and happy. It looks like she was right.

And Larry, your love and support are what allow me to fly. I thank you with all my heart.

To my clients and students, this book would not exist without you! I have received so much from each one of you, as much as I have given to you. Truly!

To Gay Walley, novelist, playwright and writing coach extraordinaire. You are a genius at seeing what is missing from a book and what will make it whole. Best of all you forced me to own up to my expertise in the field. I will be forever grateful.

To Lahr and Partners, my first agents. Much gratitude to both Jane Lahr and Lyn DelliQuadri. They went through the writing with a fine toothcomb, as many times as was necessary, to make the writing more succinct and to make me clarify what needed clarifying. Their discerning eyes have produced a much better book. And Jane, thank you for your belief in the book and its subject.

To I. Murphy Lewis, publisher of this book. Your understanding and appreciation of the subject matter, of what the babies and souls said, and of my process in bringing the material to the world makes my heart sing. It lets me know the babies will be heard. I see them clapping and laughing! They can't wait for the book to be read.

To Claudia Grotzek, artist extraordinaire. I first knew you when you were pregnant, using *DreamBirth* during our weekly sessions and then long distance as I attended your incredible home birth. I was blown away when I saw your artwork. My heart is dancing, happy and grateful that you have accepted designing the cover for this book that as you put it, was called by the Universe.

To Lisa Joiner, advisor, seer, Shaman. You were recommended to me as someone who had uncanny 'seeing' ability about books and publishing. Well, you do. But more importantly you were the impetus for me to see that I could talk directly to those beings intending to come, or those that had left, and most gratifying to me, talk directly to my own guides. You validated my 'seeing', as you could 'see' exactly what I was 'seeing'—truly a gift. You taught me how to be ready, willing and able to embrace the success of my book, and of my teaching.

A book written for anyone who has been in a womb, has a child in the womb, or fervently wants a child in her womb. Those who have suffered miscarriages or had abortions will also find comfort and healing in these pages. All that is in these pages applies as well to those who parent through adoption, and those who parent through same-sex unions.

Contents

Special note from the author . . . . *xix*

Introduction *25*
       My own story: using 'soul-to-soul' talk 27

Chapter 1: The power of imagery 31
       I ask Catherine to teach me imagery 33

Chapter 2: Babies add to the "Secret garden" 37
       Babies know much more than we think 40
       My daughters, Iris and Amber 40

Chapter 3: Babies have something to say 45
       Babies know how much we are one: Mark and Elle 46
       Like your baby, you too have stories, memories,
       and a mission 49
       Lindsay 49
       Brianna 51

Chapter 4: Miscarriages 55
       Jennifer 58
       Julia 61
       The Universe talks through multiple miscarriages: Anarosa . . 64
       Sometimes the soul has a need of its own: Justine 66
       Our expectations explode: Caterina 66

Chapter 5: Abortions 73

               Isabel 75

               Shannon 77

               Paz 78

               Sophia 83

               Love is always involved 85

               Aborted babies, in essence, have their own wisdom 88

Chapter 6: Timing and choice of sex is important 91

               Risa 92

               Incorrect assumptions: Marisa 95

               Choosing your sex, and the way you come in 100

                   Naturally, through IVF (In Vitro Fertilization),

                   through surrogate, through adoption *100*

Chapter 7: Imagining your conception 105

               Patricia 106

               Guilt: not so ironclad, after all 107

               Clear veil, clean egg 109

               Gabriela 110

               They want YOU, warts and all 112

                   Mother and baby are in the same 'soup' *112*

               Body's Blueprint 114

Chapter 8: The contract between child and parents: all we need is love . .117

               Janet and Leo 118

               Shame 123

               Noemi and Mike 126

               Challenges with boys and men 129

               Talking to an emotion: chair-to-chair 133

               Lynn 136

Miscarriage 137
Taking rapists out of the body 139
Being a pair, in different dimensions. 140
Mountain lions, cougar, mother bear 141
The throat speaks .145
Archangel Michael. 146

Chapter 9:   Love softens ambition 149
The belief in suffering 150
Amily 151
Needing to be Number One. 156
Remembering the life-giving aspects of a memory. 158
Working on her attitude and relationship to men 160
To sit at the feet of God: Higher Self to Higher Self 161
Limitless love 165
Archangel 167
Amily Postscript: heart to heart 168

Chapter 10: The universe of the heart. 171
Maya, Caterina's child 172
Verification: babies hear the exercises in the womb 172
Lori's baby. 173
Galactic Marker .174

Chapter 11: How I received ovaries of light. 177
My father's illness .178
My father's death .180
Testing the imagery: my bout with cancer 183
Believing 186
    How do I know it's real, what I am seeing?
    Am I just making it up? 186
Making a different agreement 187

Contents

Chapter 12: My universe within keeps expanding 191
    The Himba tradition. 192
    Your mission is yours, not anybody else's 194

DreamBirth Exercises 199

Bibliography. 245

About the author 250

About the painter 252

to be touched

Berührt Sein

Special note from the author

The *DreamBirth*® exercises in this book are a subset of *Saphire*® Imagery. In this tradition all visualizations are called 'imagery exercises.' The majority of the imagery exercises mentioned and included in this book come from Dr. Catherine Shainberg's seminal book *DreamBirth: Transforming the Journey of Childbirth through Imagery*, published by Sounds True, 2014. A few of the exercises are now in Catherine Shainberg's latest book, *The Kabbalah of Light: Ancient Practices to Ignite the Imagination and illuminate the Soul*, published by Inner Traditions and Bear & Company, 2022. Four exercises come from Catherine's first book, *Kabbalah and the Power of Dreaming: Awakening the Visionary Life*, also published by Inner Traditions and Bear & Company, 2005. The imagery exercises that do not have a number are part of the *DreamBirth*® repertoire specifically used in the training of practitioners but they are not published in her books. Those exercises that are not copyrighted were passed down to Catherine Shainberg by her teacher, Collete Beatrice Abouker-Muscat. All exercises mentioned are included in the *DreamBirth* Exercises section. However, for *Messages from the Womb* to make sense, a short description of the exercise will always be given where the exercise is mentioned.

These exercises are more effective if recited to you out loud, so you do not have to go in and out of your dreaming mind to read them to yourself. When someone else reads this to you, you can actively imagine and truly experience the images this practice elicits. I believe this is best of course, to work alongside a certified *DreamBirth Practitioner.* (Certified practitioners are listed in the School of Images website, www.theschoolofimages.org.) Alternatively, you can listen to the second volume of the audible version of *Messages from the Womb* where all the exercises have been recorded. If you are moved to read and 'do' the exercise on your own, Catherine's book, *DreamBirth,* is the very best guide for this use. No matter which way you choose, there will be great benefit.

The work is experiential, transformative, fun

This work is experiential, transformative, life-changing, and most of all, fun. The lightness of the children, including our own inner child, awakens that playfulness, lets it blossom. These exercises not only facilitate the communication with souls, they wake-up and vivify one's imagination, one's inner knowing. Our inner child emerges and surprises with its sense of joy and creativity. At the same time, the *DreamBirth* exercises allow the healing and growing of that which is wounded within us.

This can be an active participatory book which means you will be returning to and from page to page from chapter to exercises, folding a corner, underlining.

Or you can simply enjoy reading it, taking in what the babies have said!

What distinguishes DreamBirth *from other forms of meditation and visualization?*

Why is this form of visualization so potent and transformative? First of all, the exercises are short, poetic, and fun to do. They leave room, by not being so specific with the images, for the person's own imagination to emerge. What to see, hear and feel is not specifically given, and so poetic that the imagination is sparked.

There is an art, a science behind their transformative power, and the exercises' construction. Most forms of meditation and visualization tell a story—they often describe precisely and in detail what you should be seeing and feeling. It is used worldwide even in visualizations used by athletes.

Although many of the *DreamBirth* exercises do use visualization—especially when helping the body return to its blueprint, or when helping the baby 'see' the best position for birth and so on, the exercises combine this story-telling with what can best be described as a 'jolt.' It is this jolt that allows you to slip into the imaginal, experiential mind—the "dreaming while awake" mind. The jolt can be created by an image that juxtaposes reality with non-reality, or by strong poetic language that catapults one out of everyday thinking and logic. The jolt can be created by asking a question. What do you look like after breathing with the tree? Does the baby want something in the garden that is not there?

It is in this state that the subconscious can be reached and where one's supra-conscious knowing emerges. It is this state that allows one to communicate with a baby in the womb, or with a soul that has left through miscarriage or one waiting to be conceived.

The jolt can be quite gentle, or not. In *DreamBirth,* however, the jolts are of the gentle variety, as we are dealing with a population that is already in a heightened state—pregnant mothers are sensitive to all that comes in, to all that is around them. They are easily moved—any image or act of kindness can elicit tears.

The very subject we deal with, communicating with the unborn soul can be a 'jolt.' From the very beginning—even before conception—the act of connecting with the child to be, or the child in the womb is mind blowing, and heart opening, expanding exponentially what the mind thought was possible. All that we have been taught about the separation of worlds, and the supposed 'blank slate' state of the child and their inarticulateness instantly melts away, or in some cases, explodes away when the mother or father experiences the communication from the unborn soul. It is not a small matter!

The Roots of DreamBirth

DreamBirth belongs to a rich, more than a thousand-year-old spiritual tradition. It is a branch of *Saphire* Imagery, as Catherine Shainberg names the imagery that she learned from the renowned Kabbalist, mystic and spiritual teacher, Madame Colette Aboulker-Muscat. The methods derive from early Jewish, Sephardic and Mediterranean sources; the knowledge is experiential and is transmitted person to person. In the case of Colette, her direct lineage dates back to two kabbalists, Isaac the Blind of Provence, and Rabbi Jacob Ben Sheshet of Gerona Spain, who practiced in the Thirteenth Century. Colette passed the baton to Dr. Shainberg. Colette said to her, "You are my spiritual daughter, I have been waiting for you for a long time." (Many others have learned and been greatly influenced by Colette's work.) Dr. Shainberg lived with her for 10 years, attending every class and session Colette gave from her house and garden in Jerusalem, a garden inhabited by a great Jasmine tree, and myriad flowers perfumed the house with their scent. This was where she absorbed Colette's work, and, I am sure, the experience re-awakened her own inner knowledge of the work. Colette adapted the ancient methods to meet the needs of modern-day society, and Dr. Shainberg has continued that tradition, responding to the new energies on earth.

With the creation of *DreamBirth* Imagery, Dr. Shainberg tapped into and emphasized the receptive, surrendering qualities of the Kabbalah, which literally means 'receiving.' It is this receptive quality that is so necessary to conceive and finally to birth and mother a child. As she tells us in *DreamBirth*, Colette "was famous for curing barrenness, whether of mind, heart or body, and for igniting the creative flow. She was known as 'the woman who makes babies.'"

That attribute of the lineage has exploded into the very full work we now call *DreamBirth,* with over 500 imagery exercises for conception, pregnancy, birth and early mothering. My own experience using these exercises, both as a birth doula and teacher, has very much informed all aspects of this book. And so the torch is passed from hand to hand to hand and the transmission continues, person to person!

to remember
Ginucu

Introduction

"In dream time you have been visiting your daughter in the womb, so that she can familiarize herself with your energy. You know," Patricia's guides continued, "it's all been decided. All of you have agreed to do this; yourself, your husband, your daughter and her birth parents."

These stories are true. Many of the names of the clients have been changed. A few of my clients wanted me to use their real names. What the babies said is exact!

Before I can tell you what babies have said in the womb, or what babies that were miscarried or aborted said; before I can tell you what mothers-to-be have heard from the baby ready to come into this world, I must tell my story about my own daughters.

The adventure began, and continues to unfold, through the imagery for birth and conception that I learned from Catherine Shainberg, PhD, and through my work as a birth doula.[1] Even before I learned *DreamBirth*, I met weekly

---

[1] A doula helps the mother navigate all aspects of the birth, especially the woman's physical and emotional well-being during her labor and birth of her child. A doula does not deliver the baby, that belongs to the world of obstetricians and midwives but it is the doula that attends the woman throughout most of her labor.

with each woman whose births I was going to attend. I wanted both of us to feel comfortable with each other, and of course, once I learned *DreamBirth* Imagery, and witnessed its profound effects, I found using the exercises essential. Communication with the babies occurred through the *DreamBirth* Imagery exercises.

A large number of these imagery exercises facilitate the communication between the mother and her unborn baby. The imagery is designed to do that, but as my work evolved, I realized that what truly excited me, was the communication from the babies themselves. Not only the babies in the womb, but also those who had left through a miscarriage or abortion. It was amazing, to not only hear from those babies ready to come in, but also from those who had not yet been conceived. The more I listened, the more I understood they had something to say, the more they communicated. I have learned a lot from these babies.

Communicating with babies who were miscarried or aborted happened organically, naturally. Some of the pregnant women who hired me as a doula, to help navigate the emotional and physical aspects of pregnancy and labor, had suffered previous miscarriages or abortions. Those events almost always cast a shadow over the current pregnancy, and so clearing that shadow of fears or guilt was necessary for a problem free pregnancy and birth. I was learning from experience that the births would happen with much more joy and fluidity if those 'shadows' were addressed before the birth. And when women who wanted to conceive began to come to me, it was thrilling that they were able to talk to the babies intending to come in, even before conception. Those incoming souls often have advice for the mother, or parents, of what is needed for them to be able to incarnate. And when their advice is followed, the conception success rate is phenomenal!

But the story began earlier, years before I met Catherine Shainberg.

My own story: using 'soul-to-soul' talk

*I spoke to my daughter Iris/Chu Yurong, daily, during the months after she
had been assigned to us, although we could not travel to her yet.
I whispered loving words, encouragement that we would be there soon.
I talked to her through space, in what I now call, soul-to-soul talk.*

The adoption of my two daughters from China opened the world of birth and its mysteries. I was in a session with Patricia Masters, a gifted psychic who later became a good friend, while I was anxiously awaiting permission from China for my husband and I to travel there and receive our first daughter, Iris (born Chu Yurong).

Although the Chinese government had approved the adoption when Iris was 5-months-old, they became concerned about how many babies had been adopted that year—1996—and so they stopped all permission to travel until the Chinese New Year, February 1997.

The papers had been turned in, and we were waiting to hear that a daughter had been chosen for us. During sessions, when in psychic mode, Patricia would talk in the 'we' manner. I would jokingly refer to these other voices as Patricia's people. Later, at her memorial (she passed away in 2006), I was to learn that those who talked to her, and through her, were six Tibetans of long ago. But at that point they were simply Patricia's people, who would sometimes volunteer information, and not just respond to my questions and concerns.

"In dream time, you are visiting your daughter, in the womb."

I thought I had misheard. It made no sense.

"What?"

"In dream time you have been visiting your daughter in the womb, so that she can familiarize herself with your energy. You know," they continued, "it's all been decided. All of you have agreed to do this; yourself, your husband, your daughter and her birth parents."

"What?!"

"In dream time, it has been agreed upon."

To Patricia this was a matter of fact; to me, not so much. And I pondered my traveling in Dreamtime. I began to wrap my mind around the idea that the exact daughter, the exact soul that was coming to us was agreed upon by all involved. It was no accident, this choice, this baby.

It made sense then, my feeling a great sense of connection with my first daughter, Iris/Chu Yurong, especially the day after we had officially adopted her. We were in a hotel in Nanjing, having spent the whole day at government offices, expressing our intent to be good parents to this baby, signing many official papers, and carrying around our new baby girl through that cold winter day so that she could become our daughter, legally.

Her crib was placed next to twin beds that had been pushed together. It was dark since the lights were out, sleep supposedly on its way, but I was too excited. And then I felt a palpable bridge of connection between my daughter and myself. Being a body worker and quite sensitive to energy, the strength of the connection was explosive. It felt physical. I could touch the bridge with my hands, and the words then formed, "So this is why I could not get pregnant. This is the child I am supposed to have!"

I loved finding out about my daughters from Patricia's people. I remember once asking if I had known my daughters in different life times.

> "Oh yes!" was the reply. "You have been a strong supporter of Chu Yurong in her many soapbox moments! She is a strong supporter of the underdog. You and she will be great admirers of each other."

With Amber (born Cao Zen), my second daughter, my connection was instant, before her being officially mine. When I held her for the first time the sense of love and attachment overwhelmed me.

> "You are part of the same pod," Patricia's people explained.

> "What? Pod? What's a pod?"

"In between lives you hang out together. You have done this for a long time. Iris has this type of intense connection with her father and her grandfather."

And even though I had not learned *DreamBirth* Imagery, it had not yet been developed, the rudiments of conscious *soul-to-soul* communication had begun. I spoke to my daughter Iris/Chu Yurong, daily, during the months after she had been assigned to us, although we could not travel to her yet. I whispered loving words, encouragement that we would be there soon. I talked to her through space, in what I now call, *soul-to-soul talk.*

Later I was to learn that Catherine calls this: "*talking through the ethers.*" Little did I know that I would become adept at helping other mothers talk with their babies in the womb, talk with babies that had miscarried, and talk with babies that were aborted, and that I would even help mothers connect with their babies yet-to-be.

And so, Patricia's people's dictum that I should work with pregnant women and new mothers, now makes sense to me, but at the time, I protested.

"Why me? I haven't even given birth!"

"Because you have something to offer them," was their answer.

They continued to tell me that I would help women connect with their babies in the womb and even before conception. They reiterated, "We are talking about hearing your child, for people who want to be pregnant, and when they are pregnant." They told me this in 1999, four years before I met Catherine! The truth is that idea seemed so fantastic—it did not register with me. It was only in re-reading the notes of my sessions with Patricia, in preparation for writing this book, that I actually understood the scope of it, and was shaken to my core.

At that point I felt I didn't have something to offer mothers to be, but Patricia's guides had known that I would be the impetus, the catalyst for the eventual creation of *DreamBirth.*

to receive
Anne Tarreu

Chapter 1
The power of imagery

*The stories in this book are the ones that expanded my peephole into
the mystery of creation, and along the way have buoyed my faith that
we are part of a very loving, benevolent universe.*

Let me explain to you what imagery is and how I fell in love with it. How did
I come to intuit the power it was to have in my own life and in the many lives
of those that I then touched?

If I am honest, it began very early, before I knew what it could do. It was a
strong part of my childhood. I remember, vividly, in Guatemala, sitting on the
tiled steps of our front porch. I was five. For long periods of time, I would sit,
mesmerized by the images of dancing that I would see in my mind. I had never
attended a dance concert, so I was amazed at the many dancers and costumes
I would see in my visions. The scenery in some of them came from a different
era, and I would be riveted by the beauty and complexity of the dances, the
visions I was seeing before my inner eye.

My imagination helped me retreat from the bitter and loud fighting of my
parents. The more I focused on the inner images, the softer the yelling became,

until sometimes I could not hear it at all. To this day it drives my husband crazy. I can retreat into my imagination and not hear what is going on around me. During my pre-teen and early teens, my imagination created worlds for me to inhabit.

I had two worlds that I would dip into. One was a world for only children and teens. But it was replete with stores, cars, schools, and wonderful relationships. And in it, of course, nobody yelled.

In the second world, I created a new family, with a different mother and father, who of course did not fight. And I had, instead of the one younger sister that I had in reality, four other siblings—an older brother and sister, sometimes my real sister, and a much younger sister as well. I was, of course, the favorite of each of them, and had great conversations with each one. My older sister gave sage advice, as did my older brother. We slept in bunk beds. I was wise and popular, quite beloved by the whole family. All that of course, was the stuff of fantasies, but until I turned 14, it was a rich part of my dreamfield and a big part of my reality. I spent quite a lot of time there!

It was during Alexander Technique Training,[2] that the form of imagery I am now adept in (*Saphire* Imagery), began, and led to meeting Catherine. A visiting professor of Alexander Technique came to one of my classes and suggested a very specific and quick "image." I opened myself to the suggestion. Then, something happened. Instantly my neck and back released. My whole body felt free and easy, my spine deliciously long. Astonishing! All I had done was to imagine my top vertebra moving in a certain direction, and magic happened. One quick image was equivalent to months, or in some instances, years of work. What was this imagery magic?

During my Doula training, our teacher mentioned in passing that imagery was a helpful tool to use during childbirth. When I excitedly approached her to get more information, she confessed that she had never used it herself; however, she referred me to the only book about the subject—a very small volume by

---

[2] Alexander Technique was developed a century ago by F.M. Alexander. It is aimed at improving the way the body is used, and has long been popular with actors, dancers and musicians as it improves stamina, flexibility, and relaxation. The Alexander Technique by Judith Leibowitz and Bill Connington, Harper Perennial Publisher, 1991.

Carl Jones, titled *Mind Over Labor*. I devoured the book. Although I experimented with some of its exercises, I sensed much more was possible. A few months later, at a CranioSacral Workshop, my life changed. After watching me work, one of the assistants told me about Catherine Shainberg and The School of Images. My heart leapt: a whole school devoted to the study of imagery! Little did I know what an adventure was about to begin.

I ask Catherine to teach me imagery

When I mentioned that my 'doula bag' contained learning and using imagery, their excitement was palpable. On the spot they wanted to join a class that taught imagery for birth.

In 2003, after 8 months of private work where Catherine taught me exercises to use for pregnancy and birth, she commented that if I could get a group together, the number of exercises could exponentially grow. Her creativity expanded, she explained, when she was with a group who truly wanted to learn the work. I had started to attend Catherine's group classes, and I was getting a sense of what she meant. When Catherine teaches, it's as if Spirit has an opportunity to join and add it's wisdom. Her classes are electric, deep and inspiring. Now that I teach, I too experience more creativity and inspiration when I teach a group. Spirit also joins!

The universe must have agreed. Soon after Catherine's comment I was interviewed by two premier doulas, as they needed a third back up. When they asked what was in my 'doula bag,' and I mentioned that I was learning and using imagery—their excitement was palpable. On the spot they wanted to join a class that taught imagery for birth. As one of the doulas that interviewed me had been a nurse at the birth and labor department in a major NYC hospital, she easily found others who wanted to join. This began a collaboration, of doulas and birth professionals, seven of us (although sometimes more) that continued for seven years. Our time together was vibrant and ever-expanding, like the work itself.

A combination of Catherine's expertise and genius along with our experiences in the field, created a system of short imagery exercises to facilitate, improve and address issues of pregnancy, childbirth, conception, postpartum, and early mothering. And thus, *DreamBirth* and my initiation into the mysteries of life, was born.

The adventure continues. I have, now, attended over 300 births. Through *DreamBirth* Imagery I have helped many women get pregnant, and have taught many others so that they could navigate birth beautifully without me. And now, the greatest passion of my life: I train other birth professionals in *DreamBirth* technique. The stories in this book are the ones that expanded my peephole into the mystery of creation, and along the way have buoyed my faith that we are part of a very loving, benevolent universe.

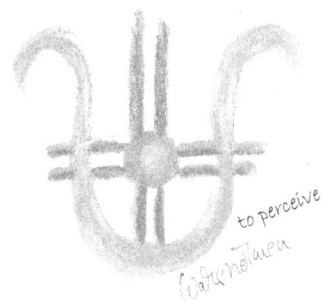

to perceive
(wahrnehmen)

Chapter 2
Babies add to the "Secret garden"

And Julia's baby, besides wanting orange flowers and a stream,
told her mother to use the stream to wash herself of doubts.
"Wash your doubts away,"
the baby repeated.

I will begin by telling the simple stories of what babies in the womb suggest they want in the imagined garden that their mothers (or fathers) create in preparation for the birth.

I teach every pregnant woman I work with, and those who are trying to get pregnant, the *DreamBirth* exercise called the "Secret garden," and I usually teach it early on. It calms and rejuvenates, it helps women connect and harmonize with nature. This is especially important for someone who is pregnant, or trying to get pregnant, and for those pregnant, it begins to set the stage, the imaginal setting—where the birth will take place.

The exercise is simple. And although it is always more powerful to 'do' an exercise, the following description of the "Secret garden" exercise will put in context the baby's answers. The exercise begins with an induction used in all the exercises, "Close your eyes. Breathe out slowly three times, counting from 3 to 1, seeing the numbers in your mind's eye. See the number 1 as tall, clear, and bright." The exercise then asks you to imagine being in front of a circular walled garden. When you reach the gate and unlock it you describe what you see, smell, hear in this garden. And of course, if the garden needs tending, or changing, you do so, until the garden is the way you want it. It is a wonderful introduction to the power and creativity of this type of imagery: here you can fix or change anything that is not to your liking! And you can do it quite quickly! Once you go deeper into the garden you find a tree that attracts you, you go to it and when there, you are asked to breathe in harmony with nature in the garden, until you feel rested or rejuvenated.

As a practitioner, each person's garden reveals a lot about the person and her current state. Some gardens are very colorful and wild, others are very manicured and orderly; some have vegetables, some need tending, some are quite large, others small and intimate. The variations are endless and unique. But the garden exercise is also a wonderful way to start to communicate with the baby in the womb, or even with the baby not yet in the womb, and to appreciate the uniqueness of each soul, as each soul seems to be very specific about what they would like added to the garden. The "Secret garden" exercise is not written to include communication with the baby, but one day, after hearing the very rich and luscious description of a client's garden and how rejuvenated she felt, on impulse, I asked her to take her eyes down to the amniotic sac, and imaginally ask the baby if there was anything else it wanted, or whether the garden was perfect as it was. The response surprised both of us, the baby said, "Pebbles!"

Since that incident, I always check with the child in the womb, if there is anything more they want. And if the child has not yet been conceived, we invite the child into the garden, so they too can tell us what they would like. Although some are very happy with the garden as created, many have something to add, very specifically. Here are a few of the responses:

My client, Serene, an interior designer with a preference for a neutral palette was quite surprised when her daughter, in the womb, wanted orange flowers in the garden. It was not a color she particularly liked, but was so struck by the desire that she put in many orange flowers, until the baby was happy. Interestingly, as the couple moved into a new home and needed to re-decorate, I noted that she put orange accents in the baby's room, and in fact, some orange pillows in the living room!

Babies have asked for blankets to lie on, dogs, cats, swing sets, a sibling, and many ask for water in the garden and so fountains, ponds, streams, rivers, then become a part of the garden. One baby wanted a lot of fish in the pond, again orange. Colors do affect us in different ways, and orange is the color of the second chakra, the energy center that is indeed the nexus of female creativity and birth. Try imagining a bouquet of orange flowers in the area of the womb or lower belly. How did that make you feel? In looking over my notes I was struck with how many babies asked for orange!

But Melinda's baby wanted to add pink roses to the red roses and yellow tulips that were there already. And then the baby showed her mother an image of water lilies, and so a pond with lilies became a permanent part of the garden. Marisa's baby wanted balls, as well as yellow flowers and a fountain. Miranda's baby wanted a bowl and something soft to lie in; and closer to the birth, the baby wanted his mother to relax! Ashley's baby wanted butterflies. Kevin and Catherine's baby had very specific messages for each of them. He wanted his very active mother, a dancer professionally, to know that it was "okay to rest," and that he loved her. He told his father that he did not like snowboarding, does like dancing, and wants more music. He also wanted his father to remember the feeling the father had about floating in the womb! And Julia's baby, besides wanting orange flowers and a stream, told her mother to use the stream to wash herself of doubts. "Wash your doubts away," the baby repeated.

Once, when working with a couple very close to the day of the birth, each parent constructed an imaginal garden, to prepare for the oncoming birth. The father's was quite wild, "like an English garden," and the mother, who was a lawyer, imagined one very manicured and orderly. When they asked the baby if anything else was needed, the child asked for the father's garden to become more orderly, and wanted the mother's garden to be 'wilder!'

Babies know much more than we think

Iris was in advance preparing herself and me for the arrival of a sister.

But I have jumped the gun! The particular path my *DreamBirth* work has taken could not have happened without two experiences, each with my two adopted daughters. They taught me that children know much more than they should at a very, very early age. I had no idea at that point, how early consciousness begins, and how far back each of us can travel.

My daughters, Iris and Amber

The first experience was with my eldest, Iris. She was very late to talk, her very first 4-word sentence was not uttered until she was four-years-old. Although my husband despaired that she would ever talk, I knew by how she ordered her crayons in rainbow order, by her fascination with letters and numbers, that she was highly intelligent and would talk. I was right. Not only did she learn to speak, but also was an Honors student at college.

Yet when we spent the summer in Maine, when Iris was 18-months-old, there were no words on the horizon. We had already put in our adoption application for a second child from China, and I had been told it would take a while, so I was not expecting a phone call from the adoption agency, for at least another six months.

On one of our trips into the supermarket in Brunswick, a supermarket that included a video rental section, Iris found the video aisle, and pulling me along, picked out an Elmo video, "There's a New Baby in My House." She looked at me intently and handed me the video, her way of saying, "Please get it for me."

And so, I did. Iris watched that video every day, sometimes twice a day, for the two weeks we were allowed to keep the video. I assumed it was because of the last song in the video; a very lyrical song sung by a soprano, Iris's preference in vocals. When it was time to return the video, Iris indicated she was not ready to let it go, so for two more weeks Iris watched that video. Finally, it was time to return to New York.

Much to my shock, the week we returned, I received a phone call from the adoption agency. Our second daughter was ready to be picked up! Iris was in advance preparing herself and me for the arrival of a sister!

Amber, my younger daughter, showed me children are aware, and in the recesses of their mind, remember what happened the day of their birth. Amber, as many infant girls in China, during that time, was abandoned in the wee hours of the morning at a busy square, the day of her birth. As the doctor from the adopting agency explained to us, babies are abandoned in areas that will soon fill with people; that way they can assure that the baby will be picked up, usually by a police officer who then takes it to an orphanage. Often the person leaving the baby will stay, hidden, until they see the baby is picked up.

When Amber was 18 months, the four of us went to Montreal, part vacation, but primarily where Iris could receive Auditory Integration Therapy, from the person with the most experience in North America, Dr. Binet. For 10 days, Iris and I went to the doctor's office, where for half an hour in the morning and half an hour in the afternoon she would listen to music through highly calibrated earphones. The music she listened to was designed to exercise or desensitize, where needed, every part of her 'hearing.'

During the therapy, Larry, my husband, spent time with Amber exploring beautiful Montreal. At the end of one of those afternoon sessions, Larry appeared at the building, looking ashen. And then he told me what had happened. He had spent the half hour with Amber, looking at the fancy shops in Montreal. Amber had got out of the stroller and was pushing it herself. She could hardly reach the handle bar. Pushing with all her might, a gigantic grin on her face, Amber continued, until she suddenly stopped, took her baby-doll out of the carriage, put the doll on the sidewalk and ran off.

Larry swooped in, picked up the doll, brushed her off, and said, "No, no. We don't put the baby out in the street." With the doll now safely tucked under the blanket, Amber resumed pushing the stroller, then again abruptly stopped, put the baby on the sidewalk and ran off. Larry says she repeated the sequence the whole time they were there, about 10 times.

Larry looked at me, "Do you think she knows?"

"Apparently," I responded.

Not only did a part of her know, she knew about the emotional connotations. Once, when she was three, and I had just given her a bath and dried her, she turned to me, still wrapped in a towel, and asked, "Was I angry when my mother put me on the street?" We had never had a conversation about her adoption story, except to let her know that she was adopted and came from China. Jolted by the question, I thought about Amber's incredibly passionate personality, and answered truthfully, "Knowing you, Amber, you most likely were!"

That same year, while Iris was in Kindergarten, Amber and I went to do some shopping at the local supermarket. She had her doll with her, and when we arrived at the house, as I was carrying the shopping bags, Amber followed me, but then abruptly put the doll on the sidewalk and ran off, looking very intently at me.

I put the shopping bags down, very deliberately picked up the doll, and said, "Well if nobody else is picking the doll up, I will. I will take care of her." Amber, with her eyes on me the whole time, ran back and grabbed the doll from me!

Very soon after, during our nighttime ritual, when Larry and I would take turns tucking each girl in and reading her a story, Amber would hold me and say, "I miss my Chinese mommy." I would hold her and whisper, "I know." And would hold her until she either fell asleep or she changed the subject.

Interestingly, she never did that with Larry. I am not sure if it was because she knew he would feel very upset, or because I was, in effect, the other mommy. She repeated this ritual daily for a week or two; and then one afternoon, while waiting for Iris's bus to arrive, I said to her, "Amber, I know you miss your Chinese Mommy, but I am so glad you came to me!"

Without missing a beat Amber replied very matter of fact, "Don't worry, Mommy. I want to be with you."

unity
[illegible handwriting]

Chapter 3
Babies have something to say

*"Even though we appear as individual entities
or expressions, we are ultimately one."*
—Mark and Elle's baby

I have found that all babies know what is happening and have something to say, even earlier than my Amber did. It was a surprise to the mothers and myself that babies in the womb can be quite articulate.

Not all mothers can hear what the child says in the womb, but they will 'hear' the baby in images, or feeling tones. There have been women who 'hear' their babies in words, as we understand words and I am particularly fascinated by what they say. All mothers, however, respond to the baby's communication, whether it is in words, images, or sensations.

Babies know how much we are one: Mark and Elle

All of us need to be acknowledged, to be taken into account, to be appreciated.

Babies get advice and help about how living in our dimension will be different than where they are. By the husband of a lovely client, an explicit view of the differences in the world of the unborn and our world, the world of the born is given to us.

Elle had come to me first as she was pregnant. She continued working with me after she suffered a miscarriage. She trained with me in *DreamBirth* as well.

Wanting to conceive again, Elle and her husband regularly 'talk' to the babies to be. There are two of them, they were told. They want to come in together. Elle's suspicion is that her miscarriage was partly due because the little girl wanted to come in with her brother, who wasn't quite ready to come into the world. In one of their communication sessions, Mark, Elle's husband, was given a 'tour' of what it is like for the babies in their dimension. They have named their children to be, Michael and Juliette.

Here is his report of the experience:

> "I came into the Garden and a portal opened up. And they took us (Mark and Elle) to a portal.
>
> Mark continued, "And basically I lost my body when we went in there; we both didn't have bodies anymore. Michael said to me, 'This is how we are. So, when we come, even to visit you in the garden we put on a form, but this is who we are. And this is who you are. We are actually one. Even though we appear as individual entities or expressions, we are ultimately one.'"

That is why the communication from the inside, and the baby, is often fast and fleeting, and the more experience one has with this type of communication the 'louder' it seems to get. And so, people who have worked with imagery have learned how to pick up the images, feelings and words that are 'sent,' and do less editing and censoring than someone who has less experience. In the beginning of this work the image is too fast, or the person doubts it is a communication. They may feel it is perhaps something they are 'making up.' The baby and one's inner knowing communicate not just with images. The communication is with all the senses and emotions. Sometimes the parents will receive the communication in images and feeling tones, and sometimes they will hear words, telepathically.

It is the parent's reaction and response to hearing their baby communicate that truly transforms the relationship. This communication from the womb may change the parent's and even the baby's view of life. Inside the mother is a complete human being with opinions, feelings and wisdom. Inside her is a baby that responds to her, a baby that can express what she wants in "the garden," and who may even give the mother a specific suggestion, "Please drink more water." More transformative is when the baby responds to the images the mother is seeing or creating in the *DreamBirth* exercises. It is one thing when the mother 'sees' that when she drinks the cool spring water, in her imagination, she has become transparent. It is another when the baby comments that the water feels cool and that the mother is now transparent! The baby can see and feel what the mother is experiencing in her imagination, and that moves the relationship to another level.

In such a dialogue, the relationship and perceptions of each other expands exponentially. It is one thing to know you have a live human being inside you, but it is something else to experience the baby inside as already having thoughts and opinions.

I see the mothers' amazement and connection when they tell me what the baby said it wants or what the baby shows them it would like. The feeling in the room palpably changes, not just for the mother, but for me as well, and I suppose radically for the baby. Here is the parent—the parent, which the baby has deliberately chosen—asking the baby their opinion. Not only do we not think of babies inside the womb having full consciousness,[3] but also now we are being asked to consider this being's opinions and feelings.

---

[3] Pre and Perinatal Psychology are founded on this belief. *Your Baby Remembers* by Rita Kluny, RN, has a good summary of the birth of Pre and Perinatal Psychology, Chapter 8.

All of us need to be acknowledged, to be taken into account, to be appreciated. All of us need to be seen for the full beings that we are or can become. Being seen and heard helps us blossom fully. It is well known that even plants do much better when acknowledged and appreciated. It is said in the Talmud, that God whispers lovingly to every blade of grass, "Grow, grow. You are wonderful, grow!"

Once at a birth, I was with a client who had the most visible, majestic contractions I had ever seen. Her belly literally took on the shape of very powerful rhythmical ocean waves. Without thinking about it, I whispered to her, "Wonderful, wonderful, perfect contractions. You are incredible. They are bringing your son down and out. Perfect. They are perfect!" A week later, during our post-partum visit, she told me that even though she felt she really had no control over her contractions, it was so healing and empowering to be told how perfect they were, and how wonderful she was! It made her feel that the baby would be out soon because of how perfect her contractions were! Her feelings were correct; the baby was out soon!

One of my favorite stories from Masaru Emoto,[4] who demonstrated vividly that water responds to words and music and the intention behind them, is an experiment that was performed by hundreds of families in Japan, inspired by Emoto's findings. Three jars of fermented rice were treated quite differently: One jar was given many words of love and appreciation, another was yelled at, insulted, told how ugly and stupid it was, and the third jar was completely ignored. Not surprisingly, the jar of fermented rice that was treated with words and thoughts of love stayed sweet smelling, did not decompose at all. The bowl that was yelled at did not do as well, but did better than the bowl that was ignored. The ignored bowl grew putrid very quickly.

The moral of that story is clear: treat living things with care and love, and pay attention to them! This may be why some children perhaps provoke their parents or others, so that there is at least some response from them, but that is a subject for others to write about!

---

[4] *The True Power of Water* by Masaru Emoto, pages 96–97. Beyond Words Publishing, 2005.

Like your baby, you too have stories, memories, and a mission

Acknowledging the baby's full consciousness and uniqueness seems to create a mirror for the mother.

As the mother realizes that the child in her womb is unique and has a consciousness, it occurs to her that she too had a consciousness when she was in her mother's womb. The pregnant mother begins to have memories and begins to understand the stories from her own mother when she was pregnant with her. The perception and understanding that the pregnant woman is also unique, worthy of acknowledgment and appreciation, spontaneously appears. She was herself in a womb, fully conscious and feeling, like the baby inside her now. And that perhaps she, too, not only chose her parents, but had a mission, a purpose to incarnate in that family, or in the world at this time. The appreciation for life, and experiencing more fully its mystery seem to grow when the communication with the baby is concrete and specific, and that perception heals many perceived hurts. Instead of seeing that the pregnant mother came into a difficult family situation as part of her victim-hood, she starts to wonder why that choice was made. Did she, like the baby inside her, decide to be born to her parents out of excitement, out of a sense of hope? Perhaps she could see that there would be an opportunity to grow. Perhaps she chose her present parents to change the familial pattern of suffering. Or is the suffering part of what she signed up for, part of what will polish and shine her, and bring out good qualities, like perseverance and compassion? The binary view of good and bad, of victim and lucky one, seems to expand, to get less binary, less either/or when the mother is in dialogue with her own baby in the womb.

Lindsay

Lindsay was both very fluid with the imagery and could hear the baby talk from the very start of our work together.

Lindsay saw me 5 times over a period of about 7 weeks to learn *DreamBirth*. The last time she saw me was when the baby was at 34½ weeks. Her baby was breech, that is with her head up near Lindsay's heart, instead of down, near the birth canal. When we did the "Turning Baby" exercise, she said it felt difficult imaginally to turn the baby, so we went inside, imaginally again, of course, and asked the baby if there was anything we needed to know about the situation.

The baby responded, "I get dizzy."

Many times, a present problem has what we call 'ancestral roots.' There are events, ideas from the past, or from the distant past—passed on from generation to generation, that are influencing the present scenario. Imagery is a beautiful tool both to discover the ancestral influence and to mitigate and change the effects—if needed.

I asked Lindsay to go back inside and see if there was an ancestral component to this situation and to see if there was something we could help with. Our 'dreaming' self has access to our fuller and greater knowledge. Lindsay went in and saw a ship on its way to America. "I'm being shown my grandfather as a three or four-year-old boy. He is there with his mother who is pregnant. I see both of them throwing up." She heard as well, "Your child has the same gene as your grandfather. They easily get dizzy and nauseous."

I asked Lindsay to find out if the gene could be 'tweaked,' that is changed, so that her child would not be so prone to dizziness and nausea. Lindsay responded immediately. "I just saw hands of light do that. Even before you asked." Lindsay then opened her eyes and reported that she was feeling a lot of movement from the baby.

Her doctor had told Lindsay that after the 36th week, a C-section would be scheduled if the baby had not turned. We went in one more time to talk to the baby, asking the baby if she would be in the right position by the 'deadline.' The baby's response was, "If it feels good."

I got an email from Lindsay about a week later, after her checkup that the baby had turned. She went on to have a vaginal birth. This is the email I received from her a very short time after the birth of her daughter:

> *"I was in early labor for 2 days, active for about 12 hours. Pushed for 2.5 hours. Not easy, but well worth it :) The imagery was VERY helpful. I'll tell you a funny story about the doctor next week—she was being very pushy—and I stood my ground, and then used imagery to open up my cervix. It was cool! Be well. See you soon.*
>
> *Xoxo,*
>
> *Lindsay"*

Brianna

"That is an issue between you and your mother. That won't be an issue between us. That is not what I am coming in for."
—Brianna's baby said in the womb

Brianna could also hear her baby.

Brianna herself had a rather contentious relationship with her mother. They got along, but Brianna did not feel truly connected to her. There was a reason for this, according to Brianna. Brianna was the second child. She never met her older sister, who died of cancer at two-and-a-half-years-old. Brianna always felt that she lived under her dead sister's shadow, that she could never be as good as the beloved first daughter and that consequently her mother had never fully accepted her. Perhaps the pain of having loved and lost a child made it difficult to completely take in another child. In any case, a feeling of connection was lacking.

Brianna was understandably nervous about how her relationship with her daughter, now in her womb, might be affected by this. She feared that her relationship with her daughter might also be lacking.

I suggested she check in with the baby. Her baby was loud and clear, "That is an issue between you and your mother. That won't be an issue between us. That is not what I am coming in for."

Interestingly, Brianna did decide to invite her mother to the birth. As the hospital only allowed two people in the room with Brianna at a time, Brianna decided that she would have the two people she needed most at the time. The groupings varied, sometimes I was there with Brianna's husband, other times with Brianna's mother, and sometimes I was out of the room. I was ushered in whenever she felt an exercise would be helpful, or when my expertise would be calming. We all agreed to not be offended when one of us was asked to leave the room.

I was with Brianna in the room, after she had decided to have an epidural, so that she could relax and concentrate on the imagery.[5] There is a time during a woman's labor, where she is most vulnerable. She needs her head stroked, her hand held. Although I was in the room leading her through a few imagery exercises, visualizing her baby coming down and out, I was moved to stroke her hair every once in a while. I could feel her mother very much wanting to be of help. She, too, was feeling the pull to 'mother' her daughter. According to Brianna, whether it came from her mother, or from her own reaction, her mother had never 'mothered' her. Brianna had taken care of herself. She could not remember her mother being physically affectionate with her. Or possibly Brianna had never let her.

Brianna could feel her mother's desires and her trepidation, trepidation because she did not want to get Brianna upset. After all, this was new for both of them. Brianna signaled to her mother to come next to her, and gave her, in effect, permission to touch her and comfort her. The shift in the room was palpable.

---

[5] An epidural is medicine, given intravenously, that numbs the nerves in the pelvic area, so that the pain of the birth contractions is considerably reduced or relieved completely.

Brianna indicated to me that I should leave and ask her husband to come in. I did so, feeling moved about what had just happened between Brianna and her mother. And while I was in the waiting room, filled with the memory and sensation of the shift that had just occurred between Brianna and her mother, her husband flew into the waiting room to inform me that they were about to take Brianna in for a C-section. It was totally unexpected; the baby had been doing beautifully. Apparently in my short absence the baby's heart rate went dangerously low and, as they could not bring it back up, they decided the only safe thing to do was to take her out by caesarian.

I was shocked; everything had been going so well. As I rushed in, I reminded Brianna to see all the doctors in light, and to talk to her baby. I kept saying this as she was being wheeled to the Operating Room. Although Brianna's husband and mother were shaken, Brianna was calm and unperturbed. I told them I would wait to see them after the birth and went to the waiting room to ponder the events. It almost appeared that her mother would be forced, to continue taking care of her, as she had moments ago, for what may have been the first time in Brianna's life. When I saw them a few hours later, Brianna's daughter happily breastfeeding, and Brianna quite joyful, I could not get that thought out of my mind. A week later, I broached the thought to Brianna, as, indeed, her mother had moved in for a few weeks to take care of her. Brianna had had the same thought. It felt like Brianna's newborn daughter engineered the emergency so that Brianna's mother would move in and care for the two of them!

wisdom
(Weisheit)

Chapter 4
Miscarriages

Often a miscarriage occurs to nudge the mother into necessary improved behavior, or at times to awaken in her the intense desire to have a child, and sometimes to allow the mother to experience her humanity, or to open up a deeper conversation of having a child, with her partner.

Being able to talk to the soul of the miscarried baby changes everything for the parent. Listening to what the babies have to say about why they left, and whether they are coming back, greatly expanded my view of the universe. There is always a positive reason why the baby leaves, as you will see in these narratives. Often a miscarriage occurs to nudge the mother into necessary improved behavior, or at times to awaken in her the intense desire to have a child, and sometimes to allow the mother to experience her humanity, or to open up a deeper conversation of having a child, with her partner. The reasons are specific and unique to each mother, family, and child. Recently I read of a baby leaving the body because it would not be healthy[6] and it wanted to be in a healthy body.

---

[6] *Spirit Babies: How to Communicate with the Child You're Meant to Have* by Walter Makichen, Bantam Press, p. 98.

Doctors often assume that the main reason a baby miscarries is because the DNA is not exactly right, that the fetus will not be able to develop normally, and so the fetus naturally miscarries, that it is a natural, physical self-correction. However, in my experience there are many other reasons, having to do with getting the parents ready for parenthood. According to Walter Makichen, a clairvoyant who specializes in talking to 'spirit babies,' sometimes the soul is not quite ready to come in; it has trepidation about the sex it is choosing, or about incarnating at all.[7] I agree and have seen many times that a miscarriage acts as both an annunciation that the soul is ready to come in, and as a gentle warning to please get things in order. Sometimes the soul says it is planning to come back, other times they tell the mother another soul will be coming. The soul will often explain why they are not the ones coming back, if the mother asks. This answer can be painful for the mother, as they want that specific child to come back. Yet I am always amazed at the love that must exist for a soul to be willing to come in for a short time, knowing that it will soon leave. The purpose seems to be a service to the mother, to help her move in the direction she needs: to eat healthier food, to be happier, to realize she has more love to give and can have a second child, and so on. When the soul is not planning to come in, it still seems to definitely have a bond with the mother or with the next child that is coming, or to both. The miscarried souls have a strong message. Each one of us seems to have a great network of helpers, and that one person's 'helpers' can easily communicate and co-operate with another person's helpers! And of course, if the soul says it is planning to come back, all systems are a go for the mother! It is easy then to ask the soul what the mother needs to do for the child to return, and the mother is very motivated to do what is needed. And when the mother is impatient because she has not yet gotten pregnant, the child to be will often assure her all is well, that he or she is coming.

What the mother needs to do, according to the child, is not always a 'doing.' Currently I am working with a mother who desperately wants to be pregnant, even though she does not have a willing partner. She has been in the process of doing In Vitro Fertilization Treatments (IVF), and in the first treatment, to her great happiness, she got pregnant; sadly, she miscarried soon after. Although her

---

[7] *Spirit Babies: How to Communicate with the Child You're Meant to Have* by Walter Makichen, Bantam Press, p. 98.

doctor was encouraging, her second IVF treatment was not successful. As she was deeply discouraged and doubtful that she would become pregnant again, I suggested we call upon the soul of the miscarried child. The child said she was planning to come back, but that she needed a mother who could play with her.

My client explained: "I don't play much, I never did. I grew up in the Soviet Union, and all I did was go to school and do homework. On my day off I went to a camp where I also did homework." She describes her present role as always being the responsible one, needing to take care of her parents' affairs as their English "is not strong." She could not remember ever playing.

If you feel you had a very unhappy childhood, the memories of unhappiness are all too readily available, and all those that do not serve that underlying belief seem to recede from consciousness. In my late 30's, when I read *The Nature of Personal Reality* by Jane Roberts,[8] I came across the idea that even in the most miserable of lives, not every experience in that life is miserable. That made sense to me. I was convinced that my early life was quite unhappy and I had been a poor little rich girl who was never seen or listened to. All my available memories proved that point.

My higher self must have been itching to get me to discard my woe-is-me point of view. I began to accept the idea that there was not only one kind of experience in my life. I spontaneously started to remember very happy times playing with my cousins and sister, and tender moments with both of my parents, and many with my grandparents, and particular aunts and uncles who had a great fondness for me. In a short time, the tapestry of my childhood memories changed considerably. I could call upon both very happy memories as well as not so happy ones. The picture of my life, of who I was, changed before my eyes. Perhaps I was not the victim I so firmly believed I was.

Assuming my client had played sometime in her childhood, I had her go back in time, first in her imagination, to the very first time she saw herself playing and being happy, and continue from that memory to the present. For homework

---

[8] *A Seth Book: The Nature of Personal Reality* by Jane Roberts. Bantam Books.

I had her make a list of everything that gave her pleasure. The change in her memories mirrored mine. She remembered how she and many of the girls played with paper dolls after doing their homework, in the dull, strict communist, after-school center. She remembered how her aunt said she was always skipping and dancing.

She decided to start having as much fun as she could now in her present life as an adult, and promptly took herself and a friend to see the ballet. She began to see her life through a different lens, not as problems she needed to fix and take care of. Her intuition was telling her to wait a while before she tried another In Vitro Fertilization treatment. She was wise. I was sure her future child wanted her to truly integrate pleasure and playing in her everyday life, and for that more time was necessary.

Jennifer

Jennifer's daughter told her she was waiting for Jennifer to really want her.

Another mother who could hear her baby very clearly was Jennifer. Her daughter was quite chatty in the womb! Years later, when I asked permission to tell her story, Jennifer relayed that her daughter was still talkative. Jennifer also opened my mind to the world of miscarriage.

Jennifer could 'hear' her baby, but not at the beginning. I first saw Jennifer because she had just had a miscarriage and was understandably very upset. There are *DreamBirth* exercises that help with the grieving, and there are also exercises facilitating conception—which was Jennifer's intense desire.

Jennifer was responsive to the grieving exercise, but could not really 'see' or 'hear' very much until we did one of the exercises to prepare for conception. It is an exercise "Cleaning your Bedroom," where you imaginally clean your bedroom very thoroughly—vacuuming, dusting, mopping, airing out the rugs, clearing every corner and getting rid of all that is not needed. You re-arrange the furniture, if necessary, and then add something of beauty to enhance the room.

When Jennifer opened her eyes after that exercise she said, "That was very different. It was the first time I saw so clearly. All colors became very bright and the walls became a beautiful yellow gold. And it was the first time I could see where to put the baby and all the things it needed. When I was pregnant I had not been able to visualize where to fit the baby in our one-bedroom apartment."

Jennifer looked at me, "Do you think I miscarried because I wasn't ready?" At my suggestion, she went 'in' imaginally to talk to the soul who had been miscarried. She asked the question. The answer was, "Yes," and the soul continued, "It was also so you could feel and understand how much you want a child." Jennifer asked the soul if it would be coming back. The soul said she was.

I have worked with many women who suffered miscarriages. The answer to this question is very specific. If the soul says it is not coming back, it will tell the mother what its purpose was (if the mother asks.) If the same soul is intending to come back, it will say so and tell the mother what may be missing for the soul to incarnate again.

Jennifer's daughter told her she was waiting for Jennifer to really want her. Jennifer saw the image of a baby with wide-open arms, reaching out to her. Jennifer did get pregnant again after about a year. We realized that the new child's birthday was almost identical to the day that the miscarried baby's birthday would have been.

During this second pregnancy, Jennifer was able to actively 'hear' her daughter. It was the first time I witnessed that. (Since Jennifer, I have worked with several mothers who can actually 'hear' their unborn babies.) During her second trimester, Jennifer would walk by a small fountain with many goldfish. Her unborn child would comment on their beauty and movement. "I love the fishies," she would tell her mother.

I couldn't wait for our weekly session to hear what the baby had said. In the third trimester Jennifer was very busy at work, feeling pressured and tired. During that time, she did not hear the baby. She could only hear when she was truly relaxed. Once, when taking a break at work, at her boss's insistence, with her feet up, and browsing through a *House and Gardens magazine*, she heard her daughter say, "When we live in a house with a yard like that, my brother will come."

At week 32 or 33 her doctor told her the baby was breech, it was not head down. Jennifer tried imagery and acupuncture, getting more and more upset that the baby was not turning. As the baby had not turned by week 35 we began to rehearse the birth with two scenarios, the one she had been rehearsing "Rehearsing the birth—the flower"—seeing the baby come out of an open flower—and then the cesarean version "Cesarean." She imagined being in a beautiful garden, with people she loved and who loved her, and then seeing the doctors with hands of light and instruments of light doing the operation perfectly. Before rehearsing this version, we asked her body and the baby if they were willing to co-operate, and both were very happy to.

Jennifer was insistent she did not want to plan the date for the C-section. She wanted to come to the hospital when her labor started. She wanted her baby to be born when the baby indicated that it was ready, when labor began. After much negotiating and promising that she would come to the hospital right away, the doctor acceded to her wishes.

About two weeks before the birth, Jennifer came in to see me looking very relieved. "I heard the baby say, 'I don't want to swim like a fishy.'" She did not want to swim out the birth canal. After that communication Jennifer practiced the birth, the cesarean way, in the garden. Understanding that it was her baby's choice made all the difference to Jennifer. When her labor began, she called her doctor and me, so that I could lead her again through the birth rehearsal, the cesarean way. As predicted by the exercise, the operation went beautifully, and with *DreamBirth*'s exercises to help with the healing, Jennifer was up and moving, carrying her baby in much shorter time than the doctor's expectations.

Although the world of miscarriage was revealed to me first by Jennifer, it was with Julia that I witnessed the whole arc of a miscarried soul that came back to the same mother.

Julia

"Use the stream to wash your doubts away."
—Julia's baby

Julia hired me, as doula for her second pregnancy the minute she found out she was pregnant. I had been her doula during the birth of her first son. She was a lawyer in a high-powered law firm and her logical mind, at first, was quite dubious of the imagery. How could pictures in your mind, as she put it, do anything? She became a believer when she was able to change her son's position during labor using a *DreamBirth* exercise, and avoided a cesarean.

For the second birth, Julia was ready for the imagery, and so we began doing *DreamBirth* exercises, right away. The first exercise we did was "Going into the womb to visit your child," an exercise that I always use. It promotes bonding, and lets a woman very quickly experience her 'inner sight' in the exercise. You let your eyes travel to the womb, and 'see' the baby in its watery environment, and you tell the child anything you wish. In subsequent visits, you remind the baby of what is developing that week, and how beautifully it is developing. Julia, however, was having trouble 'seeing' the baby; something that had not been the case in her first pregnancy. And sure enough, at around the 8th week, I got a phone call. Julia was hysterical, she had just come from the doctor, and they could not hear the heartbeat.

In a half hour she was at my office. Julia very willingly went into the *DreamBirth* exercise, "Entrusting Your Baby to the Holy Mother," which begins simply, after breathing out slowly three times, "See the soul that has left your body and ask it to show you in images or tell you what made it go away, and what if any corrections need to be done for the soul to be able to return." We didn't go further, Julia began to smile broadly, her mood lifted instantly.

> "She's here. I can feel her. She says, "I love you, and will come again!" Julia was ecstatic.

> "Julia, ask the soul if there is anything that you need to do to help her return?"

Julia saw an image of herself, her husband Vlad, and her son Ryland at the playground.

"What does that mean to you?" I asked.

"That I need to have more fun with them, as a family we need to play more."

Julia beamed as she left my office that day. "Claudia, I can feel her presence. I can really feel her!" From the first moment Julia connected with the soul, she knew it would be a girl. The journey, however, was in no way over. It took Julia many, many months to get pregnant, and being the worrying type, she often lost faith. But as soon as she would calm down, in our sessions, and connect with the soul, she would hear, "I'm here, mommy. I'm right here, you just have to be patient." The wait afforded Julia time to resolve issues with her son and her husband, so that the image of all of them having fun together, in the playground, would become reality.

The first issue that presented itself was with her four-year-old son, Ryland. He was picked up from daycare by Julia's parents, and then Julia would come to pick him up at their house. The problem was that Ryland did not want to go home, he preferred to stay at his grandparents, and if truth be told, as much as she loved her parents, Julia was a little hurt.

And so, we did a very simple visualization: we called upon the higher self of Ryland to appear, and asked him directly why he wanted to stay at his grandparents. He showed his mother the image of an early morning ritual, making coffee. He told her he wanted to be part of the family; he wanted to be included, to be able to help.

I asked Julia what this was about. She explained that it was often a conflict for her, between Ryland and constantly looking at her phone, responding to the work demands of the corporate law firm she worked for.

The repair was straightforward. Julia decided to give herself an extra 20 to 30 minutes so she would not be rushed, and she decided to put away her phone during that time. The morning routine now included Ryland helping her to make the coffee. She also decided to give Ryland more uninterrupted time when she was with him, no more glancing at her phone. That was all it took! The next session Julia reported that Ryland was now quite excited to see her when she came to pick him up, and easily went home. And yes, the three of them—Ryland, Julia and Vlad—were spending a lot more time at the playground!

Still, there was no pregnancy. When she would come to our session, despairing that it would never happen, I would lead her every time to connect with her daughter to be. "Be patient, mommy. I am here, I am coming," was often the answer. To give herself hope Julia would often visualize her future child, a girl with long hair that Julia would carefully and lovingly braid. That image came to her again and again, giving her great solace.

One time when Julia was truly distraught, her daughter said, "I am ready. Pray so that you know things happen for a reason." Julia had seen cherry blossoms every time she did the exercise to clean her womb, an exercise we did right after the miscarriage "Shining your ovaries and uterus." And indeed, in the spring, when the cherry blossoms were in full bloom, Julia did get pregnant! Neither she nor I had known why the cherry blossoms kept appearing!

Her daughter continued to give wonderful advice while in the womb. When Julia was very worried about the results of the genetic test she had taken, to determine whether the baby had Down syndrome, we did the "Secret garden" exercise to help her calm and re-connect with nature, and to hear advice from the very wise apple tree that had a central place in her garden. The apple tree's advice was, "Hush, don't cry, everything will be okay." And when we asked the baby for her input, she said to Julia, "Use the stream to wash your doubts away." The baby was referring to the stream in Julia's imaginal garden.

Soon after this, when the cherry blossoms were in bloom, Julia knew she was pregnant. We worked on possible sibling jealousy; *DreamBirth* has wonderful exercises that prevent it or at the very least, reduce it greatly. They are very effective. At the end of one of our sessions Julia confessed that Ryland had said that he wanted to wear a dress and wanted his hair to grow so it could be braided. Her Russian parents and husband were getting quite upset. "How about you, what do you think?" I asked.

"I think that is how he wants to be in life, that is his orientation in life, which doesn't bother me. It bothers my parents and my husband." The image, however, was striking to me. Ryland seemed to want everything that Julia had been imagining for her yet-to-be-born little girl.

An exercise clarified matters. In imagery we called upon the higher self of Ryland, as we had before, and asked him why he wanted to wear dresses. "Because girls are loved more," was his answer. That problem was easy to remedy. Through the ethers (mind to mind, through the imagination), she let Ryland know how much he was loved. Interestingly, after that exercise, Ryland no longer wanted dresses or braided hair! We did as well "Talking to a young child," so that Ryland could experience the deep connection and love his mother had for him. In the exercise the child goes to a cloud, to the moon, to the stars and is shown the bridge of love that exists between the child and the mother, no matter the distance.

The Universe talks through multiple miscarriages

Some of us can take a gentle hint; others need to be hit in the head before listening. Sometimes it takes more time to 'fix' what needs fixing, or it may be multiple things we need to work on and so multiple nudges are needed.

Anarosa

"I am the same baby inside you now! You were not quite ready.
I am coming here to teach you about love."
—Anarosa's baby

Anarosa was pregnant and had already bought the CD of the basic *DreamBirth* exercises because she wanted to do the exercises that were not in the CD, and deal with her guilt and fears with me. And so, in our very first session, we delved into the subject of her three miscarriages, before this successful pregnancy. She knew there was a *DreamBirth* exercise for miscarriage, and was very open to doing it.

We looked at the first miscarriage. Following the *DreamBirth* exercise "Entrusting your baby to the Holy Mother," we asked the soul what its purpose was. Anarosa also asked if it was the baby inside her now, and if not, if it was planning to come back.

The soul said its purpose was, "To wake you up, to start taking care of your body." It told her, "I am not the baby inside you, and I'm not planning to come again, my job has been accomplished."

I asked Anarosa if indeed she had changed her physical habits. "Yes," she said. She had started to eat regularly and pay more attention to the type of food she ate, opting for real food instead of snacks. As a programmer in the financial industry, her job had required her to be on call, and to put in many late hours troubleshooting. She asked her company to switch her to a less stressful, more normal hours position. Luckily the company was able to do that.

The soul of the second miscarriage also said it was not coming back to her. They were together in another lifetime, but would not be in this life. This soul's mission was to get Anarosa to start to love herself, and to connect more with her partner. I asked Anarosa if the soul had succeeded. "Yes! But I still have a way to go with loving myself. My husband and I did become closer, though." "How?" I asked. Anarosa explained, "We both listen to each other's point of view more, and I now feel he really understands what I am going through, much more now than before that miscarriage. He can feel my pain and respond to it with compassion."

And then we called forth the third miscarried soul. "I am the same baby inside you now! You were not quite ready. I am coming here to teach you about love." And then Anarosa imaginally focused on her baby in the womb, an exercise she did daily. Anarosa reported, "He has a big smile and he's waving!"

Sometimes the soul has a need of its own: Justine

"All I wanted was to be loved in the womb."
—a miscarried soul

It was Justine's communication with her miscarried child that deeply moved me. I had assisted Justine during the birth of her first daughter, and she came to me for the pregnancy and birth of her second. She had suffered a miscarriage in between. We went in to talk to the miscarried soul.

When Justine asked her if she was planning to come back, the soul's answer was that she wasn't. The soul continued, "All I wanted was to be loved in the womb," and the soul reassured Justine that the soul in her now was the one slated to be her daughter. The miscarried soul had received what she wanted and came for, to be loved in the womb. That is all she wanted to experience.

And so, the soul, which is served by a miscarriage varies from pregnancy to pregnancy. Sometimes it is the mother who needs to learn something, sometimes the family, and sometimes it is the soul itself!

Our expectations explode: Caterina

"When I come to meet you on earth."
—the baby often said

Caterina's story shows how miscarriages and abortions can be interwoven and interconnected bridging generations.

I met Caterina over Skype in June 2014, when she was 14 weeks pregnant. As she had attended one of Catherine's workshops and had a private session with her, I felt a little apprehension; would I 'pass muster' with Caterina? Would she feel that working with me would be worthwhile?

Very soon into the first session, both her apprehension and mine dissolved (indeed she wasn't sure she would want to work with me after having loved her session with Catherine). We both got into the work: as I see it, the work is about truly connecting with the baby, and then going about discovering and clearing negative beliefs not only about birth, but about life.

I see, time and time again, that clearing the negative beliefs not only helps birthing greatly, but also helps mothering itself. If you are convinced that everything you do turns out badly, for example, that belief will affect your birth, and very likely your ability to mother. Or you may be convinced that it is not possible to deal with contractions unless you have an epidural, or perhaps that childbirth is part and parcel of the suffering of womankind, and that it cannot possibly be a good experience, and whoever says otherwise is lying. Or you may believe that everyone in the medical profession will not listen to your needs, or that they only have their reputations in mind. All of those types of beliefs will have an impact on the nature of the birth the woman and child experience.

The work is not linear; it weaves in and out as the necessity presents itself. At that point in my practice, I knew that exploring the terrain of beliefs about birthing and life is an integral and necessary part of the process of having a successful birthing and mothering experience. Exploring the beliefs helps the mother free herself from negative beliefs and patterns she learned from her family. Sometimes inherited 'gifts' are wanted, and helpful, sometimes, they are not!

By the time I worked with Caterina I not only understood the power of imagery, but also after many births (over 200 at that point) the road to a successful birth experience was becoming very clear to me. Just doing the pregnancy and birth exercises does not work if there are prominent underlying fears and anxieties, or an unstable physical environment. The environment can be compromised by worries, not enough money, stressful relationships, and so on.

The body will not open easily if there is great fear about life or the present situation. Why should it? Two messages are being given at once: "Open, it's easy. Your body is fluid and flexible." And at the same time, "No, don't! It's dangerous out there! I don't know what my husband will do, whether I will lose all my freedom, whether there will be enough money, and so on."

On our very first meeting, I discovered Caterina was almost 45-years-old, and she had had two previous miscarriages. Interestingly, and probably to her benefit, the age of her first miscarriage, 42, is what stuck in my head, and allowed me to be much more optimistic about her pregnancy and the outcome of the birth process. I had worked with many 42-year-old's who had fairly easy births! My 'mistake,' that is, deciding that she was 42, allowed life to teach me something: a 45-year-old could have an easy, uncomplicated pregnancy, too. Whatever fears and doubts I harbored stayed out of the way, and I operated as if she were 42!

As is customary, the first *DreamBirth* exercise I give is "Going into the womb to visit your child." Caterina, in her imagination, went down into the womb, to look at her child, and to tell her baby anything she wanted to. After the experience, Caterina reported, "The baby is so happy! It's waving its hands and is smiling!"

Her main concern was that she worried a lot. She had always done that, and then she told me about the two miscarriages she had had, the first one in 2011 when the fetus was 6 weeks, and the second one in 2012, which was a very early induced miscarriage. "I am trying to be relaxed and calm," she told me, "but I can't help worrying. It's different for my husband. He is Muslim, is younger than I am, and he always seems serene about what happens. The worrying is part of my family," she elaborated. "Both my mother and grandmother were great worriers."

Caterina was very open, and very much wanted to deal with her two miscarriages; they weighed on her, and it contributed to the worrying about this present pregnancy. And so, in imagery, she called upon the soul that she miscarried the first time. The soul revealed in words that its purpose was, "to show you that things can be easy, but it wasn't the right time." And the voice continued to say, "I love you very much," but that the soul was now 'free,' and was not planning to come back.

Caterina elaborated on the importance of that message, as she had always felt her life was very difficult. That first soul emphasized that Caterina 'deserved to have things come easily.' And that pregnancy at age 42 had happened very easily, with no medical assistance. A true gift. That message was given to Caterina in many ways: when I first taught her "Holding the tree" exercise, the message that the tree had for her was, "Relax, be happy."

During the following weeks Caterina practiced the normal repertoire of *DreamBirth* exercises. The baby looked very happy when she went in to visit her, and she especially loved going into her 'Secret garden' imaginally, where the baby had specifically asked for "a blue blanket to lie down in." As the sessions continued, Caterina felt especially connected to her baby and would often report the baby smiling and waving her hands. In one exercise she saw the baby 'clapping' in response to an exercise.

It was not until about the 7th session, shortly after a visit from her mother, that I detected a change. She did not feel as connected to her baby, and felt a little hurt that her mother was not excited about the baby. "I don't think I can love anybody else like I love you," the mother confessed.

And then out came more details about her second miscarriage, which had been a molar pregnancy, and had to be induced at the hospital.[9] Her mother came to stay with her during the procedure, and it was then that she found out about her mother's abortion, which Caterina had always been told was a miscarriage.

Caterina's situation starkly contrasted with what her mother had experienced in Italy, many years ago, where abortion was illegal. Caterina's mother felt that she couldn't keep the baby because Caterina had been born with one leg shorter than the other and could not walk. She just could not take care of another baby. Caterina's father had never wanted more than one child. He was brought up with a brother with disabilities, and swore to himself that one child was enough. On an intuition, I asked Caterina if she felt guilty about that abortion, did she feel it was her fault that the abortion happened? The answer, not surprisingly, was that she did.

And so, we repeated the exercise we had done to talk to the soul that she had miscarried. This time she invited the soul that had been aborted by her mother,

---

[9] A molar pregnancy is an abnormal form of pregnancy where a non-viable egg implants, but will fail to come to term.

and the soul's answer was that, "All was as it should be, the abortion was supposed to happen."

The next session Caterina reported that she had been experiencing an especially strong bond with the baby. "When I come to meet you on earth," the baby often said. Memories of her own childhood had flooded her consciousness during the week. As a child, because she could not walk, she had spent a lot of time with her grandmother, her mother's mother, while her own mother went to work. "All week I have felt her presence so strongly," Caterina told me. It was especially poignant, as her grandmother had passed just a few months before.

And so, closing her eyes, breathing out slowly three times, seeing the numbers from three to one, Caterina called upon the soul of her grandmother to appear before her. She says, "I always knew you would have a child! I am always with you, and will be with you at the birth!"

To end the session, I gave Caterina "Holding the tree" exercise. I often use this exercise when advice from the inside, from the client's inner wisdom is needed. It was the same exercise we had used in our first session, when the tree told her to "relax and be happy." The exercise was leading her into the woods, encouraging her to experience all sensations as she walked deeper into the woods, and then when she came to a clearing where she can see several trees, she has to choose the tree she feels most attracted to. But instead of seeing trees, Caterina's 'dreaming' had a different idea. She saw in front of her a wall of snow, a wall of snow that was melting, and then through the melting snow she could see her old house, the one she lived in when she was quite small. It was a few meters away.

> "What would you like to do?" I asked her.

> She wanted to go into the house, and so in her imagination, she knocked on the front door, and a beautiful boy, about three or four-years-old opened the door.

> "Who are you?" Caterina asked.

> "I am your brother," he said.

They went upstairs. Now they were in her old bedroom, but now he appeared in the crib and she was in the bigger bed. She saw very specifically, a duvet cover, with a Disney theme. It was blue. She saw it in vivid detail, but she could not remember having had it as a child.

Again, she apologized to her brother. "No need to feel bad," the boy responded, "I am now the baby inside you. I am happy, now it's my turn to be loved."

Caterina opened her eyes. I had ceased writing. Caterina and I looked at each other, speechless.

Caterina did not tell her mother about the session, but a few days later she called her mother to ask about the duvet cover. She described it in detail. "Yes, you had that exact blanket when you were a baby." The guilt that Caterina had felt, low level, not even realizing she felt guilt, lifted. A weight was off. "It's pure love now, Claudia, pure love! The weight is gone, the guilt is gone!"

It was the profound love that Caterina's parents felt for her baby, Maya, once she was born, that now resonates the most with Caterina. The real confirmation for her is the incredible connection her mother has with her daughter Maya. "And my mother can be quite cold," Caterina clarified for me. Caterina's mother confessed, "I never thought I could love as I love this baby."

A few months after the birth Caterina and I connected to clarify some of the details since she knew I wanted to write her story. "The baby said to me, 'I am coming in this lifetime to be loved.' But the weird thing is that even my friends love this baby. Everybody wants to spend time with her." People stop her in the street in Italy, and that, she assured me, is not normal. "Everyone is coming to give presents, to see her, to play with her."

And then she ended, "When people see us together, they see hope! I was 45½-years-old when I gave birth to Maya, my beautiful healthy girl."

forgiveness
Kozdilei,
peoklum

Chapter 5
Abortions

"After an abortion the unborn spirit does not die,
nor does it lose its ability to create.
The womblike energy of the spirit baby world nurtures and invigorates the
returning spirit, placing it once again in a position to accept human life."
—Walter Makichen, Spirit Babies

Abortions can be more complicated. As with the previous stories of births and miscarriages, each story is unique. It is rare that a woman tells me about an abortion she has had, on our first meeting. It is only when she understands that it may impact the birth of her baby, because of the guilt she may feel, that she opens up. Guilt does not allow a woman to relax and be fluid, which she needs to be when giving birth. Particular, specific guilt does not make a woman feel whole and worthy. When a woman does not feel worthy, it makes sense to cover up that truth, it is not something that feels safe to broadcast! After all, abortion is judged harshly by many, and shame can be heaped upon those who abort. That feeling, that belief, that perception, needs to be protected, hidden, only to be discussed or shared at certain times. And when the psyche needs to cover, to protect, to hide, it affects the body. The body then does not feel free to open, to let everything 'hang out.' Birth, however, requires that a woman feels free to abandon herself to the forces of giving birth, to trust and surrender fully to the birth process, and to nature.

There are as many reasons for abortions as there are women who have them. Being in a destructive relationship, being raped, or one in which the partner does not want a child or leaves the woman are common reasons. Also common is a woman may feel it is not the right time. It can be because of school, career, age, or present circumstances. It might be because of financial issues in which money and resources may be scarce or non-existent. And in many cases, several of these circumstances co-exist.

There is more shame, more guilt and more pain with an abortion than a miscarriage, because an abortion is an active decision. And because it is often not talked about openly, and so there is isolation with the guilt and pain. Often the woman does not get to work it through with the professional help of others. The soul of the aborted child, of course, lives on; it can come back to the same woman when the situation is more suitable, or it can choose different parents. Sometimes it seems to be a decision made by all parties, including the 'other side,' and it is in fact, part 'of the plan' as you will see in Isabel's story. There are times when the aborted soul is upset, it really did want to come to the specific woman, and so must process not being able to get what it wanted.

Each one of us, just as an aborted soul, has a different temperament: some aborted souls easily move on, others need help. When a woman does want to contact the soul of the aborted child, both parties must come to a resolution. It involves the mother explaining all the reasons why she chose to abort, really communicating her situation, and of course asking for forgiveness. Often the soul has already understood the circumstances, forgiven and moved on. When that soul has not moved on, creativity and hard work are needed to bring peace to both the mother and the aborted soul. The mother may need to promise something, to always treasure life, to take care of the present child with great joy, or sometimes, if appropriate, to invite the soul back, even if this might occur in another lifetime. The resolution must be real. Both parties must be at peace, and mean what they say. In all of my cases, a loving resolution has been reached, although as will be seen in Paz's story, some resolutions take more work than others. Repair is always possible. Walter Makichen corroborates my experience. "After an abortion the unborn spirit does not die, nor does it lose its ability to create. The womblike energy of the spirit baby world nurtures and invigorates the returning spirit, placing it once again in a position to accept human life."[10] According to Makichen, once a soul has decided to incarnate, if it does not work out with a specific mother, and there is no option of returning to her, the soul will be helped to incarnate with a different mother. The environment of 'spirit babies' according to Makichen is very nurturing and almost womb like. A spirit baby is a soul who has made the decision to incarnate; it will be helped to find a new mother that fits the soul's individual destiny or life mission if the first attempt is unsuccessful. In other words, the spirit baby seems to have options if the first choice does not work out.

Isabel

"The abortion happened to bind you and Isabel together.
My job was to make sure you stayed connected, and eventually re-unite."
—the soul of the aborted baby to Tom

When Isabel entered my studio, I was struck by her tall graceful body, which at 50, still read like a dancer's body. She opened up when she realized the imaginal work of *DreamBirth* had exercises to deal with loss.

When she was 22 she met Tom, the love of her life. She got pregnant, but the circumstances were not right, and at that time she had an abortion. Shortly after that she and Tom separated, and did not see each other for 28 years.

Through a dream Tom was moved to find her; the dream told him that there was an unfinished, interrupted message. He searched for her, found her through Facebook, and was inspired to call her. By the time we met for the session, they

---

[10] *Spirit Babies: How to communicate with the Child You're Meant to Have* by Walter Makichen, Bantam Dell Publishers, p. 106, 2005.

had just recently reunited, and very soon after the reunion, Tom proposed that they have a baby together!

I asked Isabel if that was what she wanted. Inside her there was a yes and a no, co-existing. If it happened it would be an incredible gift, but on the other hand she felt she could hardly take care of herself, much less another soul.

For the moment we went with the 'yes,' and did an exercise to 'shine' her ovaries, "Shining your ovaries and uterus," and one to get rid of any ideas, emotions and experiences that prevented her from believing that a pregnancy was possible, "Clearing ancestral beliefs about conception." That exercise brought her to her abortion of many years ago. Following the exercise's script "Cleaning out an abortion," Isabel was asked to call on the soul of her lost child; Isabel saw the soul appear as a boy's red sneakers and definitely a little angry. When Isabel asked what she needed to do to be forgiven, the soul said, "Be kind to all, be receptive, have faith." When they said their final good-byes the soul added, "Receive what is being given to you, take what is offered."

Tom came in for a session as well, and when Tom called upon the soul of the aborted child the situation took on a deeper dimension. When Tom asked the child what he needed to do to be forgiven, the soul said Tom, "You need to open the 'force-field' you keep around your heart." The soul also said that the abortion happened to bind Tom and Isabel together, that the soul's job was to make sure they stayed connected, and eventually re-unite.

Tom told the soul he was very open to having a child. The soul said that if it happened it would be another soul. Three years later Tom and Isabel are still together, but a child has not yet materialized. Instead Isabel is taking the passion of her life, which is teaching in a unique field of study, to new levels. It is for her, very much so, the appropriate 'child,' the appropriate creation.

The aborted child's mission was to bind them together, and that mission is fulfilled. As Tom's dream told him, "the message was unfinished, interrupted."

Some aborted children are not so easily appeased, and have a strong message they want heard and understood.

Shannon

*"I have already forgiven you, I understand. But what I need
is for you to love this present child with all your might. You are to fully
love and rejoice in the birth of this child. I will be around
for both of you, especially my brother."*
—aborted baby's soul

Shannon was an obstetrician-gynecologist. She wanted to prepare for the birth of her son with imagery, and we got to work on that right away, as she was a month away from her due date.

She told me about a miscarriage she had suffered, but had no interest in working on it, so we went to work on all the birth preparation exercises that *DreamBirth* has to offer. It was going smoothly and uneventfully until, one day at my office, I could feel she was bothered or upset by something. "I have something I need to tell you," she blurted out. "It wasn't a miscarriage, it was an abortion."

After a pause, she continued, "I feel like the baby's spirit is following me, haunting me." She supplied the details; it was very late in her pregnancy, and it had been discovered that her baby suffered from a condition so grave that it would not be able to survive for long, and would suffer greatly. The obstetrician that attended her, and her obstetrician colleagues were advising that she have an abortion; and after what I am sure for her was an agonizing decision, as she was Irish Catholic, she did abort.

We did not need to do the exercise to invite the soul to come in, as she could sense the soul around her, even as we spoke. And so, I suggested she ask the soul why it was around her. The answer surprised us, "I am not here for you. I am here for my brother."

And then a conversation between them ensued. I invited her to tell the soul everything she wanted to, and to listen, if the soul responded, and to continue the conversation until there was a resolution.

Tears streamed down Shannon's face as she talked imaginally to her aborted child. When the tears subsided, I asked if the soul forgave her. The flow of tears resumed.

> "He says he wished I would have given birth so that I could hold him. He wanted to be held by me, even if it couldn't be for long."

> "Ask if there is anything you can do to be forgiven," I offered.

Shannon opened her eyes. "He had already forgiven me, said he understood. But what he needs is for me to love this present child with all my might. I am to fully love and rejoice in the birth of this child, and that he will be around for us, but especially for his brother."

Peace came over the room.

Paz

"I'm always with you. You keep forgetting that I never really left."
—From Paz's deceased father

Paz's aborted child was not as understanding and remained unhappy. It took some work to come to a place of peace.

Paz lives in London. She is beautiful, exotic, intelligent and successful in the music industry. Physically she is an amalgam of her parents; her mother who is half Irish and half Indian, and her father who is half Pakistani and half Portuguese.

Paz was happily pregnant when I met her, and now loves the toddler that the baby inside her has become. He constantly delights her. But Paz had had four terminations before her very wanted pregnancy. Although she had worked on coming to terms with the guilt that the abortions engendered during a session with Dr. Catherine Shainberg, the issue came up again when we started our work together.

It seemed there was more to resolve with one of them, the very first. The other souls explained that all was well, circumstances were not right, that she needed to develop more, but that they were okay, and in essence forgave her. And furthermore, not one of them was the child who lived in her womb at this time.

The first and last termination had been quite traumatic for Paz. For the first one, she had been put completely out, with anesthesia. The last one happened very shortly after her father died. This last soul explained that he had let it go, and was okay. He completely forgave her. That said, not only was she in deep mourning, but also she was discovering how destructive her relationship was with the boyfriend she had at the time of her father's death. It was the soul of the first termination that we needed to work with.

Although this first soul had originally said, "I'm okay, I've let it go," when allowed to further express itself, it had a lot more to say. To speak to the soul, I had led Paz into her imaginal garden, which this time, interestingly, needed a lot of weeding. This garden was quite different from the garden she went into daily, to talk to the baby in her womb, which was sunny, full of flowers, and quite manicured. In fact, the baby inside her had told her the sun needed to be shining, and that Paz needed to continue to rest!

To allow this first aborted soul to speak, Paz needed to weed the garden, and then once she had done so, the soul appeared. We asked the soul what else he/she wanted Paz to know, and then the soul poured out all that was needed.

He had wanted to be near her, and they took him away. He was very upset about that. "Is there anything Paz can do to make up for that pain?" At this point Paz was crying, and according to her image/vision, so was the soul.

"Does the soul forgive you?" I asked again.

"He does," said Paz. "But he wanted to be with me in this lifetime. He is still unhappy," Paz reported.

And because the thought came so strongly, I asked Paz if she would be willing, in this lifetime, to accept this soul. "Could it come to you again?" Paz paused. "Yes, maybe he can come again, because this time I am with a different man, and circumstances are very different. I would be happy to have another child with the man I am with presently. I feel loved and I am making a decent living in a job that I love."

At that point the soul finally released its anger, let it go completely and was happy. "He's smiling!" Paz reported.

That was what the soul needed to hear, that there was a possibility! "Thank you!" said the soul. And then Paz opened her eyes.

Paz looked visibly relieved, and before we did "Clearing your womb," an exercise to clean the uterus of all those memories, we addressed the uterus.

In my practice as a CranioSacral[11] therapist and as a *DreamBirth* practitioner I am finding more and more that all entities, have a consciousness, whether they are souls, cells, or organs, and they will readily 'speak.' They very much want to be heard and addressed! I have experimented with this concept, both on myself and with clients, and I can vouch for its effectiveness. I got rid of excruciating plantar fasciitis pain by telling my foot how wonderfully supportive and resilient it was. Before I remembered to talk to my foot, I was in pain for three months. It is very effective. I use it with both modalities: imagery and craniosacral therapy. I first read about the concept in *Nature of Personal Reality* by Jane Roberts (A Seth Book) in the 1970s. Seth explained that we do not really need to age, that aging is simply a concept we very much believe. I liked the idea, and so I told my cells almost daily how perfect and ageless they were, and that they could retain their original blueprint. I started doing that when I was 27. When I tried getting pregnant, at age 46, the doctor told me gently, but rather directly that I was wasting my time. He would happily give me a referral to an adoption specialist. To satisfy me he would measure all the necessary hormones needed to conceive if I wanted, so I could understand that it was a waste of time to attempt conception. Both he

---

[11] CranioSacral therapy is a natural therapy that accesses the craniosacral system, the area in which the brain and spinal cord function, using a very light touch. It improves the functioning of the central nervous system, eliminates stress and enhances overall health.

and I were quite surprised to discover that I had the hormone levels of a late twenty-year-old! At this point the elucidation of the idea that cells respond to our words and thoughts is ubiquitous in CranioSacral training, both with John E. Upledger (founder of the Upledger Institute and a pioneer in CranioSacral therapy) and with Franklyn Sills (pioneer and luminary in the biodynamic approach to CranioSacral Therapy). It is a given that the cells of the body respond to consciousness and belief. I remember how impressed I was when Upledger had a 'conversation' and a negotiation with a patient's cancer cells! Both *DreamBirth* and *Saphire* Imagery addresses organs and cells; in words and in images. When I had cancer, the therapist in the hospital had me talk to my ovaries! The evidence that consciousness affects not only all living things but according to some (Kryon, Jane Roberts, Hew Len, Masaru Emoto)[12] consciousness affects objects or entities we don't normally think of as alive. Kryon often talks about the consciousness of a particular place, claiming that the knowing of what happened in the place is held in the soil. Hew Len addresses the chairs in a room before he gives a workshop, thanking them, and clearing them of any pain.

When we asked Paz's uterus if it could release all that was still there regarding the terminations, it answered affirmatively and enthusiastically, "Absolutely!"

We reconnected with the baby inside Paz, as we had before we called the other souls, and the baby had a message for Paz:

"Please remember to rest!"

Paz's baby reminded her to rest every time she went inside to connect with the growing baby! It was in this third session that Paz told me what an 'oracle woman' had told her recently: "This baby wants to be with you, has been waiting many lifetimes to do this."

It was also in this session that Paz went through the exercise "Ancestry support," one of the most important exercises in the *DreamBirth* repertoire. It is extremely

---

[12] Your Inner Physician and You by John E. Upledger, North Atlantic Books, 1997. *CranioSacral Biodynamics* by Franklin Sills, North Atlantic Books, 2001. The Nature of Personal Reality: A Seth Book by Jane Roberts, Bantam Press, 1978. *The Healing Power of Water* by Masaru Emoto, Hay House, 2004. Zero Limits by Joe Vitale and Hew Len, John Wiley and Sons, 2007. Kryon Channelings, 1997–2019, Kryon.com.

useful when preparing for birth or for any medical procedure. Whoever appears in the exercise can become part of the support and love that surrounds the woman in the garden exercise. Very simply the exercise asks you to see, besides the women around you who feel positive and supportive, all the ancestors, from the present, all the way to Adam and Eve, who are here to support you. And in fact, in many births, the beings (or souls) that appear in the "Ancestry support" exercise become a crucial part of the support during the birth. In the "Ancestry support" exercise Paz reported beautiful images, and quite a large number of supporters. "I see about fifty beings in a line, led by my mum's mum. She is first in line, very calm and peaceful."

When we asked the baby boy, inside her womb, whom he needed in the garden, he answered very specifically, 'happy grandma,' Paz's father, and about 30 to 40 men Paz did not know. As Paz's father appeared in the garden we used the opportunity for the two of them to communicate with each other. Paz had been quite close to her father, a jazz musician and a highly spiritual man. As a child she loved looking at the books and musical instruments in his study. She learned to play his guitar, and was a DJ before becoming a successful VP in a well-known record company, in charge of talent.

> "Ask your father if he has a message for you," I suggested. And as I suspected, he did!

> "I'm always with you. You keep forgetting that I never really left." Paz imagined a heart-to-heart connection between herself and her father, and through this heart bridge they continued their conversation. The father communicated that he had left to do important work, and left her here to finish the work he was doing while in this dimension. He added that the baby, her son, had a lot of work to do also, and that he would add greatly to the world.

> "You are doing a great job," he told Paz. They then said their good-byes and Paz opened her eyes. And indeed, a great job was done. Paz's little boy loves music and all those around him. He is the love of not just his parents, but of the whole extended family. He does indeed have a happy grandmother.

Sophia

Sophia did not tell me about her abortion until it was close to the birth of her child, and she realized, from my input, that it might affect her birth. As is often the case when women are having a son, issues with her father had emerged. She was the youngest of five, and apparently, the one most picked on by her father, at least as an adult. She was also the one who most resembled her father's mother. Sophia worked diligently with the imagery exercises and close to the birth she seemed to have a greater perspective and more compassion for all the people in her family. Everyone and everything were ready for the birth, including the baby's nursery! It was then, a few days before her due date, that she confessed she had had an abortion. In Sophia and her partner's case, they asked permission of the soul to abort. Here is Sophia's story, in her own words to her child to come:

> "I remember when I found out. In the doctor's office, my first time there, I had mentioned flippantly that I was a little late so I should have a test to be sure. The doctor smiled and told me how unlikely it was; she was so assured. There was only one night when it could have happened and pregnancy is not as easy as the movies make it seem.
>
> "I had always wanted to be a mother. I used to tell all my friends in high school that I wanted 5 kids. But I was not filled with joy at the news the doctor delivered that day. Everything in me screamed: it is not the time. My partner was miserable at his job and they were threatening to fire him. Debt had found him. I had anxieties and fixed ideas about what two partners need to have before becoming a family. I thought my work was too important.
>
> "And there was another problem. When we were stressed, we had fun. When we weren't stressed, we had fun. We danced and drank too much and played with drugs. I felt sure that this was not the way to start a life with you. Your father felt sure. Having you was not meant to be sloppy, accidental, dangerous, selfish, rushed, and fearful. We could not force it.

"Your father and I made a promise to ourselves that we would restart. That we would focus on creating a stable home (and body) for you to come. I went to the ocean and prayed for your return.

"I felt your male energy strongly. I named you then. We named you. I called out to you every day and every night: come back. You gave us the gift of choosing and gave us the gift of a new beginning. You let that beginning be strong, unwavering, healthy, open, peaceful.

"We prayed. We lit a candle and laid our chests to the floor and released you. We asked you to return. Your father washed my body, our body, with honey and fruit and herbs and tears. The candle burnt half way—a sign, we felt, that you heard us, that you were with us, and that you would come back. Our child, our son.

"We decided to ask for you less than a year later. It was late October and we went to Mexico. I took my last birth control pill the night before we left. We made love every day thinking of your return. We wanted it. We spoke to the ocean and knew you were on your way. The last night was a full moon. I can still see that moon, even when I am far away from it in place and spirit. It took over the whole sky, brought daylight to night. Your father likes to think you came back to us that night. It was magical and it makes for a beautiful story. And maybe you did.

"We came back from Mexico sun kissed and tired and happy. We were immediately swept into the stress of our days—work and schedules and a cold city. We only connected once in over a week. It was normal and usual and, in our bed, where we had been countless times before. By my math, that is when you came. You wanted to be home, you knew where that was.

"A week after returning from the full moon and ocean waves and deep, dark nights, I knew I was pregnant. Though there was nothing to describe; physically, I was exactly the same as every other day that came before. But there was what I can only describe as a vibration—a low and almost indecipherable hum. I went to acupuncture and the healer told me she could feel your heartbeat. I cried hearing our truth spoken, and felt your heartbeat join with mine. I went to the doctor and she told me I wasn't pregnant. The pregnancy sticks said the same.

"It was then that I learned that our path was not for doctors or chemical sticks; I never doubted or questioned. Three weeks later, everyone came together to say: Yes, I was Pregnant!

"I spent those nine months visiting you. I would dive into my belly and see your bright eyes, your dimpled laugh, your soul stretching. I loved feeling my body fill with you. I tore through past pain and cut chords that likely had stretched for generations. I worked to heal us. To love us. And we thanked you every day for your gift to us, for knowing there was another way to start our journey. I will never forget that bravery and trust—it is my guide for the remainder of my days. And it is the meaning of your middle name, Lua."

And indeed, as she suspected, they had a son. Not only are drugs and alcohol now out of the picture, but also Lua's father has a job he loves!

Love is always involved

The babies became my teachers.
"If you can imagine for a minute, what it would be like to be someone who has nowhere to go, nowhere to be and feels that nobody loves them. And only someone who can be with them like we can—what I mean is, we know we are the one that has love for them,"
one of the babies explained. Thus, they come in so the mother can experience their love.

Since my encounters with these women, I have learned more about abortion. There is great love involved. More than I realized. But my urgent question to any baby or guide that was willing to answer was: "What happens," I asked, "when a baby has been aborted, and the mother truly does not want to have a child, or that child?"

There have been several souls that have answered that question. The first soul that spoke about this came through a client who could talk for the discarnate souls, but as I got braver, I talked to the souls myself, or talked to other aborted babies through their mothers. The babies became my teachers. The answers resonated with each other: the main answer is that they do not only have one choice. I was assured that when a soul wants to come in, if their initial choice of a mother is truly not an option, they always have a plan 'B,' or a plan 'C,' or even a plan 'D,' and that they have great help in examining those choices.

Those souls that want to come in, will find a place. Some souls will wait a long time to come in with their preferred choice, even if they wait several lifetimes! In Spirit Babies, Walter Makichen affirms this.

Many souls come in to give love to the mother, especially when the mother is at a very low point in her life, and feels alone, unloved, and unlovable. "If you can imagine for a minute, what it would be like to be someone who has nowhere to go, nowhere to be and feels that nobody loves them. And only someone who can be with them like we can—what I mean is, we know we are the one that has love for them," one of the babies explained. Thus, they come in so the mother can experience their love.

This is echoed by what a client wrote to me in an email about her previous pregnancy that needed to be terminated:

> *"It was the first time I felt I loved somebody so much. Previously, I worked hard, but didn't want kids. When I felt the baby in me, I felt intense love. When my friends told me I could have a baby through a surrogate, I realized I didn't want that, because then I wouldn't feel the love I felt."*

The souls explained that although they may be upset, they never 'lose.' It is always an experience that gives something to both the mother and the soul. And the soul, they explained, very quickly returns to the light, what they call home. They are always beautiful energies, they explained to me.

> "We are here to laugh, to play. It's something the mother can still have, even if the answer is, 'No,' or 'Not yet,' or, 'Never,' or, 'Love me later.' We are always around, and it would be good to be listened to more. We are here to make your life better, less lonely. More loved."

And indeed, it was dawning on me how much all would gain by that awareness, both the mothers and the unborn souls. Clearly these souls want the mothers to feel less lonely, more loved; they want the mothers to experience their sense of fun and humor. All babies bring that lightheartedness, whether they stay on the other plane or become flesh and blood with us.

Some souls, remarkably, choose to be aborted several times.

I was a bit stunned, when I heard this from an aborted soul, first through my client who could talk for the disembodied souls, and later when I contacted the souls directly, or through mothers who had more than one abortion. "You mean many souls want to just go in and not stay, or only for a while? Several times?"

> "Well, yes. Many of us are interested in the experience itself. And we already know that the answer is 'no.' And we are still willing to go. To see what happens when they know. So, understand, we love them, and we just want to be in their lives in a way that they always will remember."

Why would a soul choose to come in, knowing it will be aborted, again and again? The answer, from several souls, was similar.

First, the souls, explained to me, it is not a death sentence to be aborted, as they instantly go back to the light. "And in the light, we are not separate, we are not abandoned." For some souls, it is a way to heal an old wound, the wound of not being welcome. Going back to the light very quickly, and several times, reminds them, drives home, that they are truly not alone, not separate at all, and quite loved. As one soul put it, "When you come in and leave through abortion, the soul returns immediately to the light. The illusion of being separate and rejected melts in the return to the light."

Aborted babies, in essence, have their own wisdom

"It is not a death sentence to be aborted, as we instantly go back to the light. And in the light, we are not separate, we are not abandoned."
—a baby soul explained

Quite recently I taught a *DreamBirth* Training to a group from Japan. All of the participants wanted to learn *DreamBirth* professionally, but a number of them were also interested in conceiving themselves. The conception exercises they experienced were therefore personally meaningful and potent. The exercise "Cleaning out an abortion," was particularly impactful. In the exercise, you call upon the soul of the aborted soul, and see the child appear as a pair of red shoes, and you tell the soul what you need to tell them, explain to them, and of course to ask their forgiveness. As I do not speak Japanese, all was relayed through a translator!

One of the women, who had not had an abortion, seemed to connect to the energy and consciousness of many aborted babies. This was what she experienced and heard:

> "I have never had an abortion, but I decided to open up to this exercise. As soon as I started it, I started crying. It was not like emotional tears, it was just very quiet but a steady flow of tears, like a waterfall. And the red shoes came up and showed themselves immediately to me. They were very beautiful red shoes. I saw instead of just one soul of a baby; I saw many souls of babies. It was like a collective consciousness of the spirits.

> "Many were talking, and I heard excuses such as, "I was not in the right place in life to have a baby," or "I was not allowed to have the baby." So many apologies and excuses and explanations came flooding from inside of me. And those spirits of the red shoes, they were not being mean and blaming, as I was. But it was more like there was a message or a teaching for me, telling me that these women needed a deeper healing. They didn't need to gain strength

to fight against, but they need to gain a real inner strength, a real inner calmness and faith. It felt like I was being given this advice and wisdom.

"So, when I asked the babies, if they plan to come back, they said, "We'll be watching from the sky, to make sure that those women have transformations." And they are not afraid, rather they are very strong and calm. And I realized that the spirits are wise and very respectful. I feel very grateful for this exercise."

wisdom
SHER

Chapter 6

Timing and choice of sex is important

"In a caesarian birth there will be no issue if the birth is for a true matter of the health of the baby or the mother. But if it is for the mother's convenience or the mother's will, the baby will have issues with its own will."
—Patricia's guides

Timing is a very tangible element in both conception and birth. It took Jennifer about a year to get pregnant, and the baby was born at about the same date that her miscarried baby would have been born. Caterina's daughter was born the same day as her father, Gabriela's daughter the same day as Gabriela's mother.

I once asked my psychic friend, Patricia Masters, if we choose our own birth dates, even if the birth is a cesarean birth. (A cesarean is planned a week or two before the estimated due date.) Patricia said we do choose our birthday, because the energy of that date will be helpful to us, and there is sometimes a long line of souls wishing to be born at a certain date, hour and year!

In a caesarian birth, Patricia's guides continued, there will be no issue if the birth is for a true matter of the health of the baby or the mother. But if it is for the mother's convenience or the mother's will, the baby will have issues with its own will. The baby might be very acquiescent or will want to exert their will strongly.

I find, no matter how strong a desire, how impatient the mother to be is, the universe has great respect for when a child wants to and needs to be born. Julia's story makes this very clear, but the first time I encountered the importance of timing was during the birth of Risa's son.

Risa

Risa not only loved the *DreamBirth* exercises, but she had actually sought me out because she heard that I used imagery in my work. Risa was a natural master in the use of imagery; she told me a story of her travels to Spain with a friend.

The women did not have reservations at any hotel, and when they arrived, all hotels were booked. After following a few false leads, Risa closed her eyes and asked for help and to be shown where she and her friend could spend the night. She saw clearly a hotel, a building near a plaza. The plaza was well known, and they easily found it. She recognized the building from the image she saw with her inner eye even though the building did not have any sign identifying it as a hotel. Trusting what she had seen, they knocked on the door. It was not a hotel, but it was the home of a family that rented rooms out to tourists, and sure enough, they had one room available!

Understandably, Risa had no problem with the *DreamBirth* exercises.

Daily she practiced visiting her son in the womb and "Rehearsing the birth-the flower." She could easily see him sliding down the stem of the opening flower, coming out effortlessly. About two and a half weeks before her actual birth, Risa called me. "I've had contractions for two hours now. I guess this is it!"

> "How are you dealing with them?" I asked. "Do you want me to come over?"

"No, not yet. I'm easily managing them."

An hour later she called me back telling me the contractions seemed to be slowing down, and sure enough, I got another call about an hour later telling me they had stopped completely. I told her not to worry. It wasn't her due date yet, and these contractions had most likely advanced the process. At her next exam Risa was 80% effaced, that is, her cervix was 80% thinned and 2 centimeters open.[13]

"Two for free," I joked.

Six days later the scenario repeated itself, but this time the contractions lasted about four hours before they stopped. She had not needed my help. At the next exam she was still 80% effaced but was open 4 centimeters. The following week, no matter where I traveled, I carried my birth bag for Risa. After all, she was open 4 centimeters, and as effaced as she was, it was clear that this was not a typical first birth. The third phone call was from Risa's mother. They were on the way to the hospital.

Risa's mother had recently arrived from the West Coast; she wanted to be present for the birth. She reported that Risa's contractions did not seem to be abating. When I asked if they were stronger than they had been, I heard Risa sound a long, long vowel during one of them. Her mother confirmed the sound by saying, "Yes, she says they are a lot stronger."

On my way to the hospital I got a call to meet them at the Birthing Center floor, as her midwife was already there. Risa, her husband, and her mother had arrived a few minutes before I did. They were not in one of the birthing rooms.

Instead they were in the entrance hallway, with the midwife calmly repeating: "Good job, baby girl. Wonderfully done!"

The midwife told me softly: "All the rooms are occupied."

Risa did not want to go upstairs to the regular labor and delivery section, as she was afraid they would not allow her to birth completely naturally. She very

---

[13] When the cervix is completely thinned and 10 centimeters open, the woman is ready to push the baby out. The cervix is, in effect, the doorway out of the womb, which understandably, to keep the baby safely inside until it is ready to be birthed, starts out at about the width of a fist, and tightly shut.

much wanted to birth in the birthing center where each room had a big tub to labor in, as being able to float in the warm water helps tremendously with the pain of the contractions. After some deliberation, the midwife decided we would go to the family waiting room which was empty and labor there. All five of us went into the waiting room with its couch, easy chairs and table. During each contraction Risa was very inwardly concentrated. She moaned softly and circled her hips as she leaned on a chair. Every once in a while, I would remind her to breathe in golden light. Her husband silently would put his hand on her shoulder or stroke her cheek.

As Risa labored, friends and relatives of another birthing woman entered our sanctuary.

"Okay baby girl, we need to find another place."

And so, we all moved to the large room where childbirth education classes are given. Forget laboring in a tub! The laboring continued—and Risa continued to be very inwardly focused, swaying and moaning—becoming water, breathing light, seeing her baby slide down. The contractions were getting closer together and stronger. The midwife checked the baby's heart rate with the stethoscope she had around her neck. "Baby is fine," comforted the midwife, "but I think we should take a look at what's happening to your cervix."

While Risa leaned on one of the tables, the midwife gave her an internal exam. "You're 9 centimeters, baby girl! Let me check the status of the rooms." Providence must have intervened as a room had just become available. Risa was starting to feel rectal pressure strongly, so the midwife checked her again. "You can't push yet, not yet. You still have a rim that I can't push back. If you push now it can swell."[14]

And so, began the most difficult part of Risa's birth. Her body had the almost uncontrollable urge to push—but she had to fight against it. The midwife, Risa's mother and I took turns looking into Risa's large blue eyes, her curly brown hair

---

[14] A woman is ready to push when the cervix, or opening, is 10 centimeters wide. Having a rim is equivalent to being 9.5 or even 9.75 centimeters. You are almost completely open, but there is still a hard part around the cervix, which is sometimes just on one side. If you push against a rim, the cervix will swell.

now matted and wet with sweat, the midwife coaching her, "Blow, baby girl, blow, blow. That's right, keep blowing, no pushing, blow, blow, blow." When the contractions subsided, Risa's body went limp, leaning against her husband, the bed, or one of us. She was getting tired.

For ninety minutes we helped Risa not to push. Every half hour the midwife checked Risa internally. The rim was still there and would not budge. Meanwhile I was imagining pouring warm sunlight, trying to melt that rim. I visualized the midwife's fingers full of light. I talked to the cells of her cervix. Finally, at the third exam the rim disappeared. "Okay," she sighed, "let's push!"

After five pushes Risa's son emerged and was placed on her chest. Her son, not a laid-back type, made his way to the breast and latched on immediately. As Risa and her husband were taken in by the spell of their newly born son, and I was gathering my belongings, I saw Risa's mother in the rocking chair, looking at her daughter. She asked for the exact time her grandson was born. After hearing it, she said, "Risa, your son was born the exact day, and exact time, to the minute, that your brother was."

The only sound in that room was that of dropping jaws, awed by this miraculous mystery. I never talked to Risa about this 'coincidence.' I wonder now if her son and brother are very close? Did Risa have issues with her brother that she now can work out with her son? Or was the universe simply wanting to awe us with the mystery of life, winking a bit at all of us? Had I known how to talk to souls like I do now, I would have asked Risa's son why he chose that date and time!

Incorrect assumptions

With Marisa, you will see I learned not to make assumptions! This is as important in matters of the spirit, as it is with everyday interaction and communication.

If the mother does not understand the message from the baby, or needs further clarification, encourage the mother to ask again, until the message is clear. There are two assumptions in this story. Marisa's story is also about the incorrect assumption very successful women often make: that what helps in childbirth must be the same as what has allowed them to be successful in a masculine world: at all costs you forge ahead, no need to listen to what the body says, be strong, keep working hard for that is how to get ahead. The assumption is that this attitude is what will help in birth. After all, birth is a powerful, physical process. What is needed must also be powerful and physical. How could images be up to the task? Her baby's response to the imagery shattered those assumptions!

Marisa

Many times, when she would visit her imaginal garden,
we would ask the tree in her garden if it had any advice for her.
It always did, and it was often in the vein of,
"Slow down."
Another time it told her to,
"Lean on me,"
and finally in response to feeling like she always needed to excel,
she was told that she was perfect already.

Marisa is very accomplished. She owns her own company, and, like many successful women, she is used to pushing herself and to getting a lot done. Often when she would visit her imaginal garden, the tree in her garden always had advice for her. It was often in the vein of, "Slow down." Another time it told her to, "Lean on me," and finally in response to feeling like she always needed to excel, she was told that she was perfect already. Marisa loved the imaginal garden she had created; it would always calm her, and slow her down enough to allow her to hear her inner wisdom. She was learning that pregnancy and birth might not be like the normal hurdles she faced and conquered.

No matter how often Marisa practiced the "Rehearsing the birth—the flower way," (which shows the baby the ideal position for birth), her daughter was in the breech position. Marisa was getting annoyed. Why wasn't the baby turning? Marisa was 30 weeks into her pregnancy, but I explained that babies often don't get into position until week 32 or 33. That explanation did not make a dent in her attitude. Marisa wanted the baby to turn at week 30. In her work life, she was used to doing everything before it was normally expected, so why not this? She wanted all to be in order. Why couldn't the baby simply turn?

I led Marisa, and her baby, through the "Turning Baby" exercise (the same one we had used in Lindsay's story). As a good student, Marisa, followed the instructions perfectly. Much to her shock, as she was not sure this gentle work of images in your head could possibly work, she felt the baby turn. As she told me years later, it was when she felt this oceanic feeling inside of her, sensing the baby flipping, that she decided to hire me as a doula. Marisa felt the baby was clearly saying: "This way of doing things—this gentle approach—will work for me."

I had no idea at that point that she had not yet decided to hire me as a doula! I had been highly recommended by two of her friends—how could she not have decided? Again, in retrospect that was an assumption on my part.

Marisa's habitual way, and the only way of doing things, at least up to then had been to "muscle through" whatever needed to be done. It had worked well for her so far. Why wouldn't it be the same for birth? She always excelled at things. How could images be up to the task of dealing with the powerful forces of birth? In her initial thinking, imagery was not strong enough to deal with the elemental intensity that was birth. But her baby had turned! There must be something to this method. Her baby seemed to like the gentle calm that the exercises engendered. The tree in her garden made her feel loved and protected— not a usual feeling.

Three weeks before her due date Marisa became anxious. Was everything the way it should be? Was there anything else she needed to do? She was used to having everything in order, and to double-checking to see if all was correctly aligned. Although she had decided to go with this gentler approach, her desire to control was getting in the way of trusting this softer, more feminine way.

To appeal to her more masculine active side, we did an exercise where each body part was asked if it were ready for the birth, or if it wasn't, to show or say what it needed to be ready. I figured the exercise would calm her—either the body part was ready, or it would tell her what it needed. Then she could 'do' whatever the part needed. Doing something to help things along made Marisa truly comfortable.

The spine, the shoulders, the rib cage, the pelvis, the cervix, the uterus, the vagina, the hips, the legs, and the feet all declared themselves ready for the birth. There was nothing they needed! It was time to ask the baby: was she ready? The answer surprised us! When Marisa went inside and asked the baby if all was ready, the baby volunteered,

> "I'm afraid of the tight space."

> I heard, "I'm afraid of tight spaces," and so I assumed it was a generic fear. Marisa, however, had heard correctly!

Assumptions are always dangerous in communication. I had immediately assumed that the tight spaces she was referring to were perhaps from another lifetime. The baby did not elucidate further, and my assumption did not lead to further questions, so I felt we had taken care of the problem! I did not check my assumption. We practiced, "Secret garden for creating a safe space for the birth," as a vaginal birth was the desire. The baby did not mention her fear again.

And so, Marisa was able to go into labor, which she very much wanted to do. There was a scare in the early part of her labor. When the contractions started to slow down, her doctor, who knew Marisa wanted a natural unmedicated labor, suggested they try nipple stimulation.[15]

Everyone left the room, so they could enjoy the activity in private.

Marisa did not think of telling the doctor that her nipples were extremely sensitive. They were. And so, it stimulated contractions so strong and close together that the baby's heart rate began to drop. I got word that they were wheeling her to the operating room, as a C-section seemed like the safest route for the baby. Of course, by then, the nipple stimulation had stopped, and when they got to the Operating Room, the baby's heart rate was fine. As the strength and frequency of the contractions had lessened dramatically, Marisa was wheeled back to the laboring room. No more nipple stimulation!

---

[15] Nipple stimulation is an effective way to induce labor, backed by scientific research. Massaging the nipples releases the hormone oxytocin in the body, which helps initiate labor and makes contractions longer and stronger.

The three of us then settled into party mode, waiting for labor to progress naturally. It was a particularly fun labor, as both Marisa and her husband were wonderfully musical and began to sing, much to the surprise and pleasure of all, including the nurse, the doctor, and myself. It was a true concert! Marisa progressed nicely to 8 centimeters. When a woman reaches 8 centimeters, and the baby is as low in the pelvis as hers was, it is time to bring in the rolling table with all that will be needed for a vaginal birth. It is an exciting time—it means the birth is imminent.

Then the progress stopped—completely. Usually going from 8 centimeters to 10 centimeters is the quickest part of labor. When a woman reaches 10 centimeters is when she is ready to push the baby out, and often her body will naturally feel the urge to push. We tried imagery and talking to the baby, the doctors increased Pitocin,[16] and gave Marisa a lot of time—many, many, many hours—5 hours to be exact—to allow the cervix to open. The party atmosphere was waning, as the cervix was not getting past 8 centimeters. Marisa wanted to make sure that her temperature was normal. She had been in labor for two days and had been checked vaginally quite a few times, and she knew that with many vaginal exams, the temperature could rise. She knew if she went beyond 101 degrees they would give the baby antibiotics, and would take the baby to the ICU (Intensive care unit) for observation, something Marisa wanted to avoid at all costs. She asked the nurse to take her temperature—it was 99 degrees.

Finally, as there was absolutely no more progress and the baby and Marisa were getting tired, they brought up again the option of a cesarean. Marisa was more than ready. Perhaps the baby knew something she didn't. Marisa and all the adults around her knew how fervently Marisa wanted a vaginal birth. But perhaps a vaginal birth was not what the baby wanted. It was then that Marisa remembered the baby's words, "I'm afraid of the tight space." Marisa kept that thought to herself but a 'knowing' filled her. As Marisa had already dealt with the possibility of a cesarean during the nipple stimulation incident, and labor had not progressed at all, Marisa easily consented to a cesarean birth with the

---

[16] Pitocin is the synthetic version of oxytocin, the natural birth hormone. Pitocin is often given when the woman's own contractions are not continuing to open the cervix.

baby's words reverberating in her mind. She felt, in her inside, that this was the best way to go. We talked to the baby, and I reminded Marisa and her husband to "be in the garden and to see all doctors and instruments in light," as we had practiced. As is my custom, I waited until the operation was over so that I could visit Marisa and her daughter when they were in the recovery room.

Only then did Marisa tell me what one of the doctors in the operating room had told her: that she truly had a very narrow pelvis. He told her she had the type of pelvis that only 3% of women have, a *platypelloid pelvis*, where the opening is very narrow, like a coin slot. There was no way the baby could have traversed that narrow opening. It dawned on me, at that moment, that the tight space the baby referred to was not a tight space from a previous lifetime. She knew very well what was in front of her! Marisa 'knew' before she was wheeled for the second time to the operating room. What the doctor said did not surprise her—the baby had clearly told her, many weeks before.

Choosing your sex, and the way you come in

Naturally, through IVF (In Vitro Fertilization),
through surrogate, through adoption

As I knew his mother was considering a surrogate,
I asked Baby John how he felt about it.
His answer was illuminating.
"Yes, of course it is okay. Why could I not ride in another car?"
During the time he was with the surrogate, he would also be
with her (Marie), his true mother.
"I will be in my true mother's heart,"
is how he put it.
He assured her it would not take anything away from her.

Sometimes the choice of sex is very important to the soul coming in. I worked with a woman who, after several miscarriages, decided she would go by way of IVF. It felt safer and more secure.

During the first IVF, after doing a lot of personal work, we were both surprised that she did not become pregnant. While the mother mourned this event, I decided to connect with the soul to be—if the soul was willing to talk to me. In the imagery exercises the mother always saw the child as a girl. However, sometimes the sex the mother sees in imagery is not the sex of the child, simply the sex the mother is more comfortable with. I asked why the soul had not come 'in.' The soul answered succinctly. "I'm a girl. Tell my mother I am coming."

I was left to ponder her answer, and it occurred to me that in the IVF process this couple had made many viable egg/sperm combinations. In effect, at least, the doctors and technicians knew the sex for each of the frozen embryos. I asked the mother if she knew whether the embryo they had put in was a boy. She was not sure and told me that she and her husband would not ask the clinic about the sex of the embryo, as her husband was not comfortable with the idea of knowing the sex. Upon telling her what her daughter had told me, I asked her if she was willing to ask that the next time they chose an embryo could it be a girl? It may have taken some negotiating with her husband and her conscience, but this new embryo is definitely female. The baby is now happy and thriving in the womb!

I was quite aware in my work that timing (as we saw in the previous Chapter) is a big part of when a soul will come in. It was not until my experience with this baby that it occurred to me that the choice of sex can be quite important to some souls, and it may trump timing. Perhaps the souls need both the desired sex and the desired timing! Perhaps in natural conception the consciousness of the soul coming in may choose which sperm enters the egg,[17] and thus determine the sex. (In the IVF process that is not always possible, although perhaps the benevolent and loving consciousness has its ways!) Like all of us, each soul seems to have a specific sense of what is most important to them.

For some babies the choice of sex is very important, for others perhaps not as much. A pregnant woman I worked with, (as a doula for her first birth), had a very strong dream, after the birth of her first daughter, where she felt a very

---

[17] Studies from Stockholm University and Manchester University show that human eggs can 'choose sperm.' www.mancheter.ac.uk.

strong 'boy' energy. She was sure her second baby would be a boy. So was I. Her second baby, however, was a girl. I am a Facebook friend of hers and would often read stories about both her children. When the second child was around three-years-old, one day, out of nowhere, the child announced to the mother that from that day forward she would not wear a dress or skirt. What is congruous with that story is that her interests have always been what are normally thought of as 'boy' interests: she loves tools, constructing things, and seems to be quite a philosopher and a very confident human being. She likes to think about how things work. When my client posted the story about no more skirts, I couldn't help a smile, "Aah, this is the boy energy that visited her in the dream time. This is her boy." To this child, being a physical boy was not crucial.

To the soul who called himself John, the decision to be in a boy body was paramount. John first talked to me in a session with a client I worked with who was talented at hearing the souls on the other side. 'John,' as he called himself, literally burst into a session, unannounced and uninvited. He had an important message to tell me, as he knew I was working with his mother.

He introduced himself as someone that knew he wanted to be a boy. It seems that it took some work on his part to come to this decision. His mother was 'nervous' is the way he put it, and he already had an older sister and a dog. As he told me those details, I guessed his mother was a woman who had worked with me off and on, and was indeed 'nervous' whether she would be able to conceive again, and very much wanted a second child. She first came to me after having gone through many failed in vitro fertilization procedures (IVFs). With the use of *DreamBirth* exercises she was able to conceive her daughter, who even in the womb, would tell her mother to "be happy." She gives her mother the same message now that she is out of the womb!

The conception of the second baby was problematical, partly because, Baby John, as he calls himself, had not yet decided whether to be a boy or a girl, or even if he wanted to come in at all—it took a while for him to be sure he was ready to 'come in', as he put it. In the meantime, his mother, Marie, a self-described Type A personality, insisted on going through the in vitro fertilization process even when the soul had said it was not yet ready. As she put it, she wanted to make sure she did everything that could be done on her part. Marie's body, after multiple IVF tries, was suffering from all the hormones that the procedure normally requires. Her body truly needed a rest.

Baby John wanted me to tell his mother he definitely had decided he was a boy. Although I normally want all communication to be between mother and child, this time I relayed the message, so that Marie herself could dialog with the baby about this.

There was a kink in the situation. According to Marie, her husband and his brothers only produce girls. Whether this was true, I have not verified, but it was definitely a strong belief of Marie's. Baby John echoed this by saying he needed to be offered a different egg. In other words, he wanted a fertilized egg that was a boy.

In further conversations with Baby John, both with his mother and directly with me, he seemed open to different ways of coming in. As I knew his mother was considering a surrogate, I asked Baby John how he felt about it.

His answer was illuminating. "Yes, of course it is okay. Why could I not ride in another car?" He had more to say about a surrogate. He wanted to be part of Marie's family. He let both of us know that Marie would be able to rest her body, and more importantly, during the time he was with the surrogate, he would also be with her (Marie), his true mother. "I will be in my true mother's heart," is how he put it. He assured her it would not take anything away from her.

It was Baby John's communications that truly verified what I already knew from the adoption of my daughters; that a soul wants to come to a specific family or mother, and they do not always care whether it is through a more traditional biological union between the mother and the father, whether it is through donor egg, donor sperm, both donor egg and donor sperm or adoption. All modes of getting there are okay, as long as they get to their family of choice!

*to be connected
before chapter*

Chapter 7
Imagining your conception

*I always tell my students these visualizations allow one to time-travel,
change circumstances for the better in one's imagination, and then feel
the effects in present time.*

I am more and more convinced that the souls who want to come in guide their
parents to me: they want to be seen and acknowledged before they are conceived.
They are yearning to communicate and to have a say in the conditions of their
incarnation and birth. The parents are specifically, carefully, lovingly chosen. It
is a mutual choosing, as Patricia's people explained to me: the parents and the
child are all in agreement. In the case of adoption, the birth parents, the child,
and the adoptive parents are all in agreement.

The right child for you will come to you in whatever way it can. The following
story, in Creating Miracles by Carolyn Miller,[18] is one I tell my students and
clients.

---

[18] Carolyn Miller's *Creating Miracles*: Understanding the Experience of Divine Intervention, pp. 64–66.
Tiburon, CA: H J Kramer, Inc., 1995.

A woman, Hayden, had suffered four miscarriages and she eventually had to have a hysterectomy. Adoption also was proving to have its challenges, until she had a casual meeting with a pregnant, unwed mother in a Boutique. Not long after the meeting, the mom tracked her down and said she would allow no one but Hayden to adopt her baby. Essentially, she told Hayden that the baby was meant for Hayden. "This is your baby. I just know it is. It never felt like mine, and now that I've met you, I know it was meant for you." Indeed, they arranged the adoption, and when the adopted daughter, Leah, was about three, she asked her mother why she had not been able to grow inside her tummy. "I tried to come to you four times mommy!"

There is more about conception and birth than meets the eye!

Patricia

"Make room for me,"
the soul said to Patricia.
And so, Patricia began clearing her apartment of
what she didn't really need or use in order to
literally make room for a child.

Patricia, strikingly beautiful with delicately chiseled features, dark shiny hair and large blue eyes, a legacy from her Italian background, came to see me because she hadn't been able to get pregnant after two rounds of in-vitro fertilization (IVF). She was on her third round when we met, and had tried to conceive naturally for many years. There was nothing wrong physically with Patricia or her husband, according to the doctors. At 33-years-old she was the picture of health.

I asked Catherine if she could teach me imagery to facilitate conception. Her answer stayed with me.

> "It's more complex than when working with pregnancy and birth," she had explained "as there are so many factors that enter into it. Do they really want a child, or is it something they feel they should? Does the partner want a child? Is money an issue? Are there family constructs, beliefs that get in the way?"

Guilt: not so ironclad, after all

As I started to work more and more with conception, I saw that negative beliefs play a big part. For example, "Everyone in my family has trouble getting pregnant" or other similar ideas impede the process. Guilt can enter into the equation. "I don't deserve to get pregnant," or guilt about previous abortions or miscarriages can get in the way of conceiving. The thinking goes something like this: since I aborted, I will now not be able to conceive. It is my punishment.

With Patricia, as our sessions continued, the issue of a family 'curse,' emerged quite clearly. At the end of one of our early sessions, she remembered a dream— or perhaps not a dream—that had felt so real. A tall, thin, wiry man, with grey hair, stood ominously at the foot of her bed, and told her she would never be able to have children. Patricia was about 15-years-old at the time.

But there seemed to be an ancestral, familial aspect to this 'curse.' Similarly, although not a dream, a midwife had told Patricia's mother that she would never, ever be able to have children. I gently pointed out to Patricia that even though (in a dream) she had been 'cursed' similarly, her mother had been able to get pregnant as, after all, she had given birth to you! It was clear that such pronouncements were not so ironclad, after all.

That logic had escaped Patricia, a consummate Software Engineer; family 'truths' have a way of being accepted in one piece, no questions asked. Adding to the stress was that Patricia's mother blamed the difficulty on herself. Perhaps Patricia's mother's guilt and incorrect thinking lay here: she herself had been able to escape the curse, but now her daughter had to pay! When a belief is a 'family' belief, there is a very effective *DreamBirth* exercise that gets at the origin of the faulty thinking.

"Clearing ancestral trauma" exercise, taps into the subconscious knowledge we have about the origin of a familial or ancestral habit or belief system. Although it is complex, at its essence, the exercise asks to be taken to the 'origin' of the event that led to the belief system or feeling that is prevalent in the family and ancestry. For many, the original incident will emerge, and then the cords that tie everyone to that original trauma or event can be 'cut' or untangled and released and cleared.

It is the results that give the exercise credence. There will be a difference after the exercise; the person will not feel as bound, as beholden to the tenacious thought pattern as before. Catherine always admonished us to not take her at her word, but to verify that any exercise we used truly had the intended effect. Since I am by nature a doubting Thomas, I do insist on checking the outcomes. And the outcomes of this exercise never cease to astonish.

Another emerging belief that affected Patricia's well-being, and therefore impacted her attempts at getting pregnant was, "someone is trying to mess with me." As we explored this belief in imagery, familial ramifications emerged. A rift between her father and his brother showed itself as the origin, although the rift between the brothers went very far back.

Cutting cords to this event had real-life ramifications, almost instantly. Patricia had felt snubbed by her cousins, the children of her father's brother. There were family affairs that she was not invited to, even though as children they always played together. After doing the exercise, she started to be included, and if anything happened that in the past would have wounded or angered her, she no longer had the feeling that it was personal; the source clearly had to do with brothers of long ago.

When the third IVF did not work, Patricia decided she would do one last round with her own eggs (instead of using donor eggs). When that fourth round did not work, Patricia used an imagery exercise to talk to the soul of the child that was to come.

"Yes, I am coming, but do adoption," the soul said.

Patricia started to look both into adoption and donor eggs, which in her mind was a form of adoption. Especially after dealing with the two familial belief systems, Patricia's mood about becoming a mother had shifted completely from our first sessions when a definite sense of doom about ever becoming a mother was present. She would definitely become a mother, she now felt, she was just not sure in which way.

Patricia began to work on her own creative urges, wanting to create some of the beautiful visions she was seeing in her imagery. At the insistence of the soul who had said she needed to make room for it; Patricia began clearing her apartment of what she didn't really need or use in order to literally make room for a child. "Make room," the soul said.

In another session the baby added that Patricia needed to be excited and to start to envision it, at the same time that she made space for it. Patricia took this not only literally, but also decided to make it both a happy place in her house, and a happy place inside herself as well.

Making it a happier place inside her expanded to all endeavors in her life. She daily and diligently practiced "The solar plexus" exercise, which among other things, brings to you people and situations that will enhance your life and well-being. At work she began to pitch to her superiors a business idea, which they responded to. Her relationship with her husband improved and became more balanced and affectionate, and passion was re-ignited, again using a wonderful *DreamBirth* exercise "Meadow colors," designed to kindle intimacy. When the soul was asked, if there was anything Patricia needed to do to allow the soul to come to her, it immediately showed her a picture of her husband.

"What does that mean to you?" I asked.

Patricia answered, "It means to spend more time with him."

Clear veil, clean egg

Interestingly, at work she found a new friend, someone who was also doing IVF and was considering using donor eggs. She introduced her to a doctor that Patricia was very happy with, who put her on an egg donor wait list. Patricia was told the wait would take from 6 months to a year, but surprisingly (although not to me as I knew how effective "The solar plexus" exercise can be), she received the eggs much earlier than predicted. When receiving an organ from someone else, in this case, the donor eggs, it is important to clear any residues, both physical and emotional, from the new organ. Patricia loved that particular exercise, "Clearing the field of the donor egg." She saw a veil that needed to be cleared; it felt very satisfying to really clean the eggs.

Six of the eggs fertilized, and as she had seen a double helix implant in her imagery, she decided to implant two embryos at once. She felt at that point that if one of the six embryos implanted, that would be great, and if they didn't she would adopt. One way or another she was ready to be a mother. The process was not so straightforward. Her fifth try, with two donor eggs, also did not work. Undaunted, as the child to be kept communicating, she did one more round. This time, her sixth IVF, again using the donor eggs, and again she implanted two embryos. This time, and perhaps it was simply a matter of right timing for the soul, one of those fertilized embryos took. And in December of that year she gave birth to a healthy boy. I see many photos of the three of them on Facebook!

Gabriela

"You don't have to worry about me, I'm fine."
Gabriela's baby had plenty to add to the garden! Gabriela's vision
of her garden was that it was a bit overgrown, and was mostly green
with a lot of bushes. The baby, however, wanted color!
"I want red and yellow tulips, sunflowers,
and a Magnolia tree with pink flowers.
And please put in a hammock and a bird bath!"

Gabriela, a lawyer, came to me because she had gone through two unsuccessful in-vitro fertilizations and felt her body was completely failing her. A good friend of hers, also a lawyer, had engaged me as a doula, and thought the imagery would be useful for Gabriela. Gabriela felt whomever had been successful in helping her friend have a calm and positive birthing experience might be able to be successful in calming her. Here is Gabriela's story, in her own words:

> "In the winter of 2012, I was introduced to *DreamBirth* Imagery through a friend who had used it for her natural childbirth. I wasn't pregnant. I had gone through two failed rounds of in-vitro fertilization and two surgeries to attempt to prepare my uterus for implantation. The real reason I wanted a doula's assistance was because I figured if she could coach my friend through an entire

birth she could help me calm my angst. In fact, just weeks before meeting Claudia, I had been taken by ambulance to the hospital with a heart tachycardia. I felt like my body was failing me.

"I met with Claudia and soon began to learn, through visualization and breathing, to slow down my system. She talked me through listening to what my body was telling me it needed, and helped me tell my body what I needed from her. We psychologically went inside and took a good look around. For the first time in my life I was communicating with my body and really tuning in to what I was feeling. It was terrifying and liberating at the same time.

"In January of 2013, I began a 3rd round of in-vitro fertilization and used the visualizations to cope with the physical and emotional stress. I believe using the *DreamBirth* exercises and meeting with Claudia regularly was the key to helping my body become host to a perfect little embryo. I discovered a lot of emotional junk had built up in me over the years. My mother had died in 2008 and, although we were close my entire life, we were not on great terms when she passed away; I think somehow, I couldn't let go of something associated with that guilt. Claudia and I worked together for the entire duration of my pregnancy. She helped me find that place in me where my mother always lived and loved me, and I felt the support I needed from those around me, living and dead. My husband became involved and learned techniques that helped calm both of us as the birthday neared. I always knew I would have to have a C-section, and I knew that I needed and wanted the support of Claudia to guide us through the weeks leading up to the surgery. Just days before the birth my doctor informed me that she may have to remove my uterus. Claudia guided my husband and me through emotional and powerful visualizations to attempt to will my body to not need such drastic measures but to prepare my body for massive surgery and, most importantly, we learned to communicate with our child and let it know that no matter what happened it would be safe and protected. Those last few days and hours with Claudia brought me solace and peace knowing that whatever happened I could handle it and my baby and I would be okay. Claudia met us at the hospital the morning of the birth and gently guided me until they wheeled me into the operating room. I was able to continue my visualization exercises while I was without her. It so happened that I got to keep my uterus.

And, on my mother's birthday, I gave birth to a perfect baby girl."

I will add to this story what Gabriela's baby said to her in the womb. As Gabriela is prone to worry, and was, of course, worried about the baby in the womb, one of the first things her baby said when she went to 'visit' her, imaginally, was, "You don't have to worry about me, I'm fine." And she had plenty to add to the garden! Gabriela's vision of her garden was that it was a bit overgrown, and was mostly green with a lot of bushes. The baby, however, wanted more. She wanted red and yellow tulips, sunflowers, and a Magnolia tree with pink flowers. And please put in a hammock and a birdbath!

They want YOU, warts and all

Mother and baby are in the same 'soup'

What the soul wants is the connection with the mother (or father),
warts and all, more than with anybody else. Their intent this time
around is to come to these particular parents.
The baby knows the mother's 'warts.' The warts that seem
so big to the mother are not so big to the soul,
with their bigger vantage point.
After all, they see all of the mother's present life,
and often her many other past lives.

DreamBirth operates with the knowledge that the babies are affected by what the mother feels. They share the same field. Each other's emotions, feelings and thoughts, and experiences are easily and automatically communicated to the other. Mothers often suffer guilt when they feel badly, knowing it may adversely affect the baby. And they believe that if they hide the offending emotion or thought, if they could only suppress it, pretend it's not there, it would be better for the baby.

That, however, is not really possible. The baby feels the emotion even if you try to hide it, even if you try to hide it from yourself. The baby cannot help it; the baby is in the same soup. The answer is not to close your eyes to the bad feelings and suppress them, but to come to a place where they can be, at the very least released, and at the best, resolved, and transformed. Even if the mother is despairing that the offending emotions cannot be transformed, the act of confessing them seems to help in liberating the emotions, and to easily move to a different better-feeling place.

You can tell the child, "Mommy is feeling really upset now and scared. I'm afraid I won't be able to take care of you." Perhaps you might say: "I'm afraid I won't be able to do other things I want, and I don't want to resent you," or "Mommy is mad now, but not at you," and so on. The child may have a broader vantage point than the mother. I worked with a mother who was afraid she would have a bad relationship with her daughter, like the one she had had with her own mother. The daughter, while in the womb, told the mother, in no uncertain terms, that this was not the child's plan. She and my client would have a positive relationship, she told her mother.

If the child understands that the emotions or feelings have nothing to do with them or because of them, they are quite relieved. Even if the feelings do have to do with them, the fear can at least be addressed, and the child often provides a larger viewpoint. ("No, mommy. I will not be a burden. I will be a joy. You will see. I am light as a feather," was what a baby, not yet in the womb, said when her mother protested loudly that she could not afford a baby. As the mother recently confessed, now that her child is 6-months-old, she had no idea of the love and joy the baby would bring. She had had an incorrect idea about mothering.)

Admitting the emotion helps the baby/soul/child process what she (or he) is sensing. They understand where the feeling or emotion comes from, and then they can see it is not their fault. I remember when my daughter, Amber, was about three, she accused me of being mad at her. I realized I was mad, but not at her, and so I told her. She was, first, relieved that her perception of anger was not wrong (even though I was ignoring and suppressing my feelings), and once she knew it had nothing to do with her, she happily skipped off. She had no interest in listening to my explanation of why and with whom I was mad. She was happy that the anger had nothing to do with her.

Body's Blueprint

Babies in the womb seem to have a double consciousness
and so they can both feel the upset, feel the feelings of the mother,
be affected by her hormones and at the same time be able
to see the greater picture.

I recently worked with someone who had suffered several miscarriages and was currently in the very early stages of pregnancy. She started to experience bleeding and was understandably upset and in dread of another miscarriage. The ultrasound showed that the fetus was still there, its heart beating. The doctor saw that the placenta was not as solidly attached as he wished and surmised that might be causing the bleeding. Armed with this information, in our session, we created an exercise for the placenta to attach perfectly to the uterus. It was not hard to do: the body's blueprint is, after all, made in light. It is an energetic blueprint. It was simple to create an exercise where she saw the placenta, and imaginally using rays of light, firmly attached the placenta to the uterus. She decided she would visualize that every day.

We went 'in' to talk to the baby. The baby clearly said she wanted the mother to communicate daily with her. Because of her fear and sometimes upset moods, this mother had decided that it was better when she was in one of those moods to send loving entities to the baby, instead of communicating with the baby directly. And so, she sent to the baby her very loving paternal grandmother, and the baby's guardian angels, and as well, surrounded the baby in rainbow light. When she first told me she was doing this, I thought it was a sweet and generous gesture on the mother's part. However, upon hearing the baby's request for the mother to communicate with her daily, it hit me strongly that it was the mother whom the baby wanted the closeness with. She would rather have the mother in a bad mood talk to her, than have another loving entity, no matter how loving, talk to her.

What the soul wants is the connection with the mother (or father), warts and all, more than with anybody else. Their intent this time around is to come to these particular parents. The baby knows the mother's 'warts.' In fact, even before conception this soul gave her mother advice. "I want a happier garden; I need more light in the garden." (You need to avoid such heavy moods.) It had been a process of creating a lighter garden, one where both souls, the child and the mother, felt at home. It happened organically, with the mother doing her due diligence: cutting cords to unhappy experiences, making them less prominent, and remembering and focusing on happy ones. The garden was spontaneously getting to be one that welcomed both: lots of light, but also lots of protection and beauty from the trees, bushes, and flowers. The garden had a stream that both enjoyed putting their feet in, although the soul, clearly identifying itself as a girl in the mother's imagery, told the mother she did not like to dive into cold water, like the mother did!

The placenta needing to attach itself to the uterus more firmly seems like an apt metaphor for what was happening emotionally. "Please communicate with me more regularly, more firmly," is what her daughter seemed to be saying. I have found that the souls in the womb (and the souls before they come in) have a comprehensive and compassionate view of the parents. The warts that seem so big to the mother are not so big to the soul, with their bigger vantage point. After all, they see all of the mother's present life, and often her many other past lives.

Babies in the womb seem to have a double consciousness[19] and so they can both feel the upset, feel the feelings of the mother, be affected by her hormones and at the same time be able to see the greater picture. They have a bigger view. And if the mother admits, expresses the negative feeling; the baby is often able to help with a larger viewpoint and great compassion. They see the mother's greater beauty, the 'warts' to them seem to be part of the beauty of life, and they know some 'warts,' like a bad mood, are easily changeable, not necessarily a permanent part of the landscape.

---

[19] Wendy McCarty's *Welcoming Consciousness: Supporting Wholeness from the Beginning of Life*. Santa Barbara, CA. Wondrous Beginnings Publishing, 2012.

Love

Chapter 8
The contract between child and parents: all we need is love

When the child is being heard and seen,
a best-case scenario for the baby,
there is no impediment to their love.

Through this work I have learned much about the love that mothers and fathers and babies have for each other. Yet, it is the intense love that the babies have expressed in the womb that continues to stun and astonish me. I suppose the time of choosing the 'contract' between the parents and child is always a honeymoon period. It is a time when the love is very apparent. There is great excitement and a sense of great possibility for both the parents and the child; the mother has not had to stay awake night after night listening to a crying baby, unable to comfort and quiet it. The child has not experienced the mother's intense exhaustion and feelings of overwhelm. In the beginning, in all the cases I have dealt with, the love is very apparent, and is expressed by the child. I expect the love of the parents for the child, at least from those who come to work with me, but even more moving is the love of the child for his or her parents.

I am not making light when I talk about a honeymoon period; honeymoon is the correct word. When the child is being heard and seen, a best-case scenario for the baby, there is no impediment to their love. Yes, the honeymoon period can be marked by all the demands of early motherhood, but the love and the magic of this period can be recovered, if the parties are willing, again and again, surprisingly when it seems irretrievably lost. This can happen even if only one of the parties is willing! After all, love is what sets the connection in motion; it is the base line. Once I accepted that my daughters are wise and creative and responsible for their own decisions, and even now that they are in their twenties, the honeymoon period actually continues.

Janet and Leo

"Thank you, you're going to be a great mother,"
the baby told Janet.
When Janet put a drop of water on her body,
as part of the exercise, the baby said,
"I can see the water, and now you are transparent."

I met Janet and Leo at one of Catherine Shainberg's summer workshops in Europe. The first summer, Janet and Leo were jumbled in my memory with all the other people I met abroad. I do remember Janet being strikingly beautiful and tall, I remember her thin lean body, and her long blondish hair, a big smile and shiny, twinkly blue eyes. As I was about to give a short presentation on *DreamBirth,* they came to introduce themselves. It was not until a year and a half later when I assisted Catherine in a full-blown presentation of *DreamBirth,* that both of them came into focus for me.

Many of the people who attended the workshop were fans of Catherine and the *Saphire* Imagery, of which *DreamBirth* is a part. They would attend any workshop that Catherine taught. They were not necessarily pregnant or planning to get pregnant or even really interested in becoming *DreamBirth* practitioners. During one of the breaks, Janet and Leo came to speak to me. Janet looked into my eyes, held my hands, and said, "When we get pregnant I want you to be our doula!"

And six months later she and Leo did get pregnant! I was not to be a hands-on doula in the conventional sense of the word. We were on different continents, but I was intimately connected with them from that June until their daughter was born in mid-January through weekly Skype sessions where they experienced and learned the *DreamBirth* exercises. Although I was not in the labor room in person, I was with them during much of it through WhatsApp, the free application that lets you talk or video chat to anyone in the world, as long as there is Internet connection.

It is a gift to work with people who have already attended Catherine's workshops and have had private sessions with her. Their imaginations are fluid and, most importantly, they trust and believe in what the imagery can do, as they have already experienced its transformative power.

Janet and Leo had already done a lot of 'cleaning.' They understood the value of this type of imagery work, and were both willing and able to plunge in deeply. They wanted to release what might still be in the way, not only, of achieving a smoother birth, but more importantly, what might be in the way of happy parenting. They wanted their relationship to each other and to this child to improve upon their parent's relationship and their own upbringing.

And so, in June, the work began. Immediately they were off and running! At the same time that they began the communication with the baby in the womb, they dove head first into any repair that needed doing. On the very first session they did the exercise to visit the baby in the womb. The baby had messages for each of them.

For Leo, the baby had a simple message, "Have faith and trust." To Janet the baby said, "You are shining, and unicorns are playing with me." Janet said to me with great incredulity, "I love unicorns! I can't believe she mentioned them!" Janet also asked the baby about the sadness she was feeling. The baby's answer to that was direct and wise, "Let it go!"

Because of their ease and experience with the imagery I could see the baby would be able to express, through images, words and feelings, all she wanted to express, and she did! As mentioned in Chapter 3, the communication from the inside is often fast and fleeting, but the more experience one has with this type of communication, the 'louder' it seems to get. And so, people who have worked with imagery have learned how to pick up the images, feelings and words that are 'sent,' and do less editing and censoring than someone who has less experience. The baby and one's inner knowing communicate not just with images. The communication is with all the senses and emotions. Sometimes the parents will receive the communication in images and feeling tones, and sometimes they will hear words, telepathically. I have a hunch that the baby's predilections and strength of personality play a large part in the communication. Jennifer (Chapter 4) could 'hear' her baby in words, and that same baby, now an 11-year-old girl, is indeed very talkative and chatty. Once a pregnant woman who had just hired me got very unnerved by her baby's strong visual communication while doing "Weaving your child's life, tapestry and name." In the exercise you are instructed to be at a loom, and on your lap you have many skeins of colored wool. You then make contact with your child, by turning your eyes inward, and ask what color you should use. Whatever color 'pops' up is the color to use. The child inside her had a very strong sense of design, and kept 'directing' the weaving of the tapestry with much determination. The child wanted a yellow star in the middle, and a purple circle around the star. This was not what the mother wanted or liked, but no matter how much the mother attempted to weave into the tapestry the colors she wanted, the image of the star and circle superimposed itself. The mother-to-be was disturbed by this experience, and called me the evening of our session to rescind her offer to hire me. She did not want to do imagery! We easily terminated the contract and I have not seen her since, but I do remember the strength of that baby's communication. I wonder what she is like now, and if more ease exists in their relationship, or whether it is still, on both their parts, "My way or the highway."

When Janet did the exercise, "Ancestry support," she saw that the support for the baby included not only angels, but also a lot of unicorns!

Unicorns did indeed become a big theme. Without saying anything to anyone, many of the gifts given to Janet for her baby had to do with unicorns! As the pregnancy progressed, Janet's nesting and creative impulses led to her making many soft unicorn pillows, unicorn mobile hangings, unicorn paintings on the walls, unicorns everywhere! She even found a little plastic one on the ground, on one of her walks!

I sometimes worked with Janet and Leo together, and often individually had sessions so that what each one needed could receive attention. They both had had childhood trauma, to deal with, which came up first.

Janet had been hospitalized when she was 11-years-old, and had been left alone, feeling scared and abandoned. She was also dealing with the weight gain of pregnancy which was triggering eating and control issues she had struggled with her whole life: as a baby she would not take from the breast, or eat. And then she would have episodes of, as she said, never being truly fat, but being somewhat heavy. The only girl in a family of 4, she was nicknamed 'sumo' as in a sumo wrestler, by her three brothers by the time she was 8-years-old. Although her weight fluctuated, when in high school, and she was at her heaviest, she decided to reduce, and researched what she should eat to reach her perfect weight. Her mother, however, sabotaged any of her efforts at losing weight, often adding extra olive oil to recipes without Janet's knowledge. And so, fear of not being able to lose weight after the birth, became an issue.

For Leo, who was a 'surprise' baby, the experience of not being truly wanted in the first 8 years of his life, especially by his father came to the surface. He often felt guilty, and he attributed this partly to his having been born. His father had not wanted a third child. I could relate to Leo's guilt!

I myself remember a feeling I experienced when I went back to the moment of my birth, in my imagination, as part of an imagery exercise. My mother, too, felt very conflicted about my birth. Part of her wanted a child, part of her very much did not. I remembered my very strong emotion as I was being birthed, "I'm sorry, I'm sorry, I have to be born!" There was guilt for deciding to be born, for going against her feelings. I could tell part of her very much wanted the freedom of no children.

The baby very much responded to the imagery exercises they were both doing to release and transform some of their memories. The baby seemed to see and experience what her parents were seeing in the imagery exercises.

The hidden, veiled problems and concerns between Janet and Leo also showed their 'ugly heads.' As is often the case, problems that need to be resolved appear in an exaggerated form.

Indeed, shortly after they found out they were having a girl, one of the main problems between them emerged. Janet felt betrayed when Leo talked to others about the baby, feeling that he often had no sense of boundaries. For his part, Leo was mad at himself for having talked out of turn, without having checked with Janet first. The problem was a recurring one. Janet has a fairly prestigious position as a psychologist, and as the city they live in has a small-town atmosphere, she is careful as to what information is put out for public consumption. She knows that information travels fast, and she did not want any information out about the baby, at least without checking in with her first.

The experience exacerbated for Janet the lack of trust she was prone to, and which she knew had familial components. She decided to work on the ancestral and familial aspects of her sadness and disappointment, and lack of trust. She very much recognized the same feelings in her mother. After Janet poured water on her ancestry as the exercise calls for, we checked in with the baby.

> "Thank you, you're going to be a great mother," the baby told Janet.
> When Janet put a drop of water on her body, as part of the exercise,
> the baby told Janet she could see the water, and that now Janet was
> transparent.

Janet's anger and disappointment at Leo and Leo's guilt and resentment at the anger lasted a few sessions. It gave us a wonderful opportunity to resolve this deep-seated complex. As mentioned earlier, the emotions and beliefs that need to be cleared seem to present themselves in exaggerated form, precisely so they will be dealt with! Janet was feeling despair. To calm and repair this we did "Repotting the plant," a simple exercise where you repot a plant that is not doing well, into a beautiful pot with rich fertile earth. You then water it and see what happens to the plant. After that exercise, we went in to talk to the baby. Janet beamed, "The baby loves me, and is telling me that everything is alright, that I need to trust myself more."

Shame

Leo envisioned a heart-to-heart bridge between himself
and the baby; he saw it as yellow gold.
And through the bridge the baby showed him a crack on the ground,
and that it was coming together, repairing itself. The baby told Leo,
"Be with me more often, I am touching your face."

The baby had some advice for Leo as well, especially as he dealt with the guilt he was feeling for not having checked with Janet first; this only added onto other feelings of guilt he often experienced. Feelings of guilt can be multilayered. At its essence guilt speaks of the feeling of having done something 'wrong,' or that one may have hurt someone, or upset someone, whether that someone is society, the government or a person you know. The feeling can come from the still, small voice inside of us that says, "You should have defended your friend, or you should not have kept quiet." In that case it is our inside appealing us to 'right' the action, to apologize and to remedy if possible. Or the voice can be from the outside, at least initially.

Unfortunately for many of us, when young, the voice telling us we have done something 'bad' is often not that still, small voice from one's inner core, but the loud voice of a parental figure. You can be called 'bad,' or treated as if you have done something wrong, for as small a transgression as spilling milk, or of course, it can be as grave as pushing your baby sister and hurting her. And guilt can also be 'picked up' from those around you, from the collective dreamfield of your family, or even society. It is not unusual if a member of one's family is feeling they have done something terribly wrong for others to 'catch' the feeling. They may not even know what they did wrong, but the feeling is that they are guilty of something.

That was the case for Leo. His grandfather, his mother, his brother often experienced feelings of guilt—generic guilt. And so, we went in and talked to the baby. Leo envisioned a heart-to-heart bridge between himself and the baby; he saw it as yellow gold. And through the bridge the baby showed him a crack on the ground, and that it was coming together, repairing itself. The baby told Leo, "Be with me more often," and told him she is "touching his face."

Leo did follow his baby's advice, and did visit her more often, imaginally, in the following weeks. And at our next session the baby told Leo, "Please keep it up, I like how you have been visiting me."

Closer to the birth Janet and I again did the "Secret garden" exercise, and interestingly the garden had expanded, both in size and beauty. It now had a fountain with clear water, and there were many more trees and flowers, "like an English garden," Janet explained. She also saw butterflies. When we asked the baby what she needed, the request was quite specific. She told Janet, "I need unicorns. I want three unicorns; one gold and white, another one white and pink, and another one blue." She continued, "I like the butterflies to be near me and to sit on the unicorns and I like the water next to the trees, and I like the stream, but please add more violet flowers."

When Janet did the exercise to practice the birth, she saw the baby looking straight into her eyes. Janet was happily surprised to see how big the baby's eyes were!

As the birth approached, Janet's fear of not being able to lose the weight resurfaced. Due to her mother's sabotage, she had a great fear that weight was very hard to lose. And also embedded in that thought, that belief was the idea that she was not beautiful.

We did a wonderful exercise, "Clearing the office of the mind," where we rid all the instances of the offending thought, in this case, the thought and belief that she was not beautiful. When you rid yourself of that thought and all similar ones that are lurking in your mind, the exercise has you replace that old belief with new sanguine ones. And so, Janet found all the instances of both: "I am not beautiful" and "It is impossible to lose weight, I'll always be fat," all related negative thoughts. She was able to toss these false beliefs out while cleaning her "office." After getting rid of the offending beliefs, she replaced them with positive ones. Janet's replacements were: "My body can easily lose weight," and, "I am beautiful in every way, inside and out."

I had Janet connect with her baby at this point, and ask the baby if she had anything to say about this. The baby did!

> "You are the most beautiful person. I hear your heart beating in the belly. It is perfect and beautiful." And the exercise must have been effective, for when I met Janet, Leo and their baby 6 months after the birth, Janet was thin and radiant.

When fears of the actual birth emerged, the baby said to Leo: "We're going to do this together."

Janet saw her own birth as the cause of her fears, but also intuited that she needed to clear the memory and resonances of her conception. Her dreaming self, her knowing self, could see an image of her mother being very tired, with a small baby around 7-months-old. She could see her father force her mother to have intercourse, being very dismissive of her feelings. The mother cannot say, "No." She is frozen. Janet cleared the memory, releasing, cutting any cords that attached her to it. Part of the exercise is to throw the charged transformative water over all who have been affected. She could see in her images that the absolving and clarifying reached not only her ancestry, but also every cell of her daughter's body. At my suggestion she asked her daughter if she needed anything else.

The baby answered, "You did everything!"

Janet's birth took much, much longer than she expected. She was now in her 30th hour! Fear was not what got in the way, but more a supreme lack of faith. Why was the birth taking so long? She had been 'told' by every fiber of her body, by her strong intuitive voice that her birth would be like her paternal grandmother's. What went wrong? Her grandmother's birth had been two hours, that's what she'd been told.

And indeed, that is what she had come to believe, for that was true for the birth of her father, her grandmother's second birth! A month and a half after the birth of her daughter, conversationally, she was told how brave she was, going into the birth, knowing that her birth would be like her grandmother's. That is when she was first told about her grandmother's first birth, 38 hours long, exactly like hers!

In an instant her faith returned. She had been 'told' correctly by her inside, she just had no idea of the details! Having lost faith in her inside knowing and intuition, Janet told me, was the most difficult part of the birth. The actual details of her birth, the length, the pain, until she finally decided to take an epidural, were nothing compared to that loss of faith.

A piece of verification is in order here! When I met Janet's baby for the first time when the baby was 6-months-old, she did, indeed, have exceptionally large eyes!

Noemi and Mike

*Noemi saw a girl sitting on a cloud, but she seemed to be on the second tier
of the clouds, not the ones closest to her vision. She then saw an image
of herself and Mike sitting on a bench, and heard from the soul,
"Stay connected. Be together, so I feel love from each of you."*

Noemi and Mike were also quite experienced with *Saphire* Imagery, as they had attended most of Catherine's workshops in Europe. Mike, one of the organizers of the workshops, who is highly appreciative of the work says, "I credit the work with the growth of my intuitive and creative side, and in the fluidity of mind and imagination that the work engenders. I have learned that anyone can change their past, and I have truly experienced that."

Indeed, Mike's favorite exercise is "Changing the Past." He and I joke that this work, in effect, allows one to time-travel, change circumstances for the better in one's imagination, and then feel the effects in present time. Both Noemi and Mike are highly accomplished true achievers, and both suffer from the inner push that can sometimes come from needing to do everything 'right,' from needing to be 'perfect.'

Noemi, physically beautiful, is a very accomplished musician. She is, as well, a kindergarten teacher, a music teacher and was only one of three people to pass the very difficult music practicum final exam, which many attempt and fail. She worries a lot about not doing something well, but most often does it brilliantly. As Noemi described herself in one of our early sessions, she has always been a 'busy bee,' active from morning until night. She teaches a full day at kindergarten, then teaches music three afternoons, and then attends rehearsals of her singing group. She is 9 years younger than Mike and, although wise, she often feels that he doesn't always listen to her opinions, and that she is dismissed. That was one major issue she wanted to come to terms with.

Mike is a family doctor and an emergency doctor. In his practice he uses the imagery work to calm his patients. He fills himself and his instruments with light so that he achieves the very best possible outcome.

To become pregnant, Mike and Noemi asked if they could work with *DreamBirth* and me. They were aware I had helped many couples become pregnant, often after numerous attempted failures or miscarriages. But Noemi and Mike did not have such a history; it was the first time they had wanted to conceive. They simply knew that having a conscious conception, and especially 'cleaning' up anything that needed cleaning up before getting pregnant, would be better for them and the baby.

They both were very committed to unearthing difficulties and to clearing out buried material that they did not want to bequeath the child. Because of their experience and trust in the imagery work, they were courageous in bringing up issues that needed attention.

The very first session introduced some of the fears and themes that needed to be transformed, and those appeared in different iterations throughout our sessions. More importantly they connected, in this very first session, to their child (or children) to be.

As I had known them for several years, my first question to them was why did they now feel ready; why did they now want a child? Mike, about to turn 35, had felt ready for a while, Noemi 26 at that time, needed her 'ducks' to be in a row. She had just received her diploma in music teaching and had begun teaching, they had attended couples' counseling and she felt more secure in the relationship, and she had started to take physical care of herself, eating better, resting more, and she was feeling optimistic about finding a house in which to raise a child. And so, she was feeling calmer and ready to be a mother.

But one of her greatest fears about conception surfaced: she did not want a boy! She currently had an unruly group of boys in her kindergarten class. The group of ten boys, all were rude and hyperactive. Her underlying belief was that boys are bullies. It did not help that her one and only sibling, a brother, gave her parents a very hard time. As her mother would often say, "Thank God for Noemi," causing, of course, great pressure, as she always had to be good which created guilt towards her brother, for always being compared unfavorably. Being 'good and perfect' was one of the ways she could get attention.

At the end of the session I asked them to connect with the child to be, and to ask their child to appear. Mike saw a group of three kids, a girl and two boys. The girl was reaching out to him, and then the other two disappeared.

The child had a message for him, "You both grow together."

Noemi saw a girl sitting on a cloud, but she seemed to be on the second tier of the clouds, not the ones closest to her vision. She then saw an image of herself and Mike sitting on a bench, and heard from the soul, "Stay connected. Be together, so I feel love from each of you."

Before the session was over, I suggested to Noemi that boys could, in fact, be nice. Just in case, I thought to myself. I suggested she would have liked Mike as a little boy, because he was not at all a loud hyperactive bully!

Before the session was over, I knew Mike wanted to work on his anxiety. We receive many things from our parents, including labels and definitions! Mike's mother often compared Mike to her own father, who suffered great anxiety when he got a new job and new responsibilities. Not only did they constantly make that association, but also Mike's grandfather had died in a car accident when his mother was pregnant with Mike, and so there was, in a way, a double negative connection to his grandfather.

Noemi's issues, although she also suffered from the anxiety of the pressure to be perfect all the time, had a different flavor. She was terrified that she would be abandoned by Mike, and be left penniless. She knew it was not logical, but it was a persistent fear, nevertheless. It was compounded because three of the women she worked with had recently lost their husbands, one in a car accident, one through cancer, and another to a serious illness.

Noemi's fear was rooted not only in her present family history, but also in her ancestral past, as she discovered when she did the "Clearing ancestral trauma" exercise. The roots of the problem belonged to a time before she was born, although the roots were definitely re-enforced by what happened in her present life. Her parents had always had problems, and finally divorced when she was an adult, shortly after her marriage to Mike. When they divorced, each parent went back to live with their own parents, as they both lost their jobs. And so, they went from having had enough money to build a new house, to suddenly, being penniless.

But the abandonment issue went further back. Noemi had been told that when her mother was pregnant with Noemi that her father had wanted her to have an abortion. Her mother prevailed; she wanted this second child. When Noemi imaginally went back to this time, she could see and feel herself in the womb, where it felt quite safe. But the outside world did not feel safe. She could hear her parents fighting about her brother, and she could sense her brother getting in trouble. She heard her father not wanting another child, and she felt guilty, as she wanted to be born. Her desire to be born, in this case, was much stronger than her guilt at making her father feel bad. She needed to be born!

Challenges with boys and men

*As Noemi was working on her fear of boys and men, the universe
kindly intervened. Very shortly before discovering they were pregnant,
about 6 weeks after we started working together, Noemi began teaching a
much calmer Kindergarten class, with a sweet boy in the class
who was easy to love.
The boy happened to have her exact birthday!*

Noemi went further back, and could see that part of the problem came from her father's maternal side. During WW2 her father's mother, when she was five-years-old, saw her own father shot to death. The fear of sudden loss, and feeling the world is a dangerous place, had woven itself into the family dreamscape, the familial belief systems. Not only is the world cruel, but also boys and men are particularly problematic. It did not help that Noemi's mother was one of seven children, all boys with the one exception, and all her mother's brothers suffered from alcoholism.

As Noemi was working on her fear of boys and men, the universe kindly intervened. Very shortly before discovering they were pregnant, about 6 weeks after we started working together, Noemi began teaching a much calmer Kindergarten class, with a sweet boy in the class who was easy to love. The boy happened to have her exact birthday!

As we worked with the patterns they wanted to change, to shift, and with the patterns that were emerging, we simultaneously worked on the Conception exercises that *DreamBirth* offers, and began communicating with the baby to be. When Noemi and Mike went through the "Secret garden" exercise, they again invited the soul of the child-to-be to join them. Noemi's garden was very colorful with tropical flowers and palm trees. When she asked the soul what else he or she would like in the garden, Noemi saw little girls being playful and happy. Noemi took this to mean the child liked the garden!

Mike had a lot of colors in his garden, and, many, many trees. The baby's message to Mike was, "The garden needs less thick walls."

Although they found out a week later, Noemi's tropical garden was telling us that she was already pregnant! Pregnant women's gardens tend to be lush, and many have tropical plants!

The week they found out they were pregnant, they asked for a session. We did the "Secret garden" exercise again, because each time the garden can change, and this time, this is what the baby had to say about the gardens:

To Mike, whose garden did not have flowers this time, the baby asked for many colorful flowers. To Noemi, the baby asked to have Mike in the garden!

Dreams and life experiences helped put into focus those things, which needed attention. And perhaps expressed a need for a change of viewpoint. Many of the patterns were intertwined, in both of their parents and even more curiously, between Noemi and Mike. Noemi's father's parents lived with them at some point, and according to Noemi, they did not like Noemi's mother very much, and they did not respect her or her opinions. Her father only listened to his parents, never his wife.

One of Noemi's original fears and complaints was that Mike mainly listened to his family, especially to his brother and sister. She felt that their opinions mattered more to Mike than hers; and she very much felt that Mike's mother was put in that same position. Mike's father's family were the ones who mattered, and the mother's opinion did not. It was the same pattern in her own family, where her father mainly took advice from his parents, never his wife.

And so slowly as the patterns emerged, a middle ground, as opposed to a black and white view, was beginning to surface.

An incident about the choice of an obstetrician brought this black and white deep-seated attitude to the foreground again. Initially, Noemi had chosen an obstetrician because he lived near their home, but one day after Mike visited his brother and sister-in-law, who had recently had a baby, the subject of obstetricians came up. Mike's sister-in-law had done a lot of research on the subject, and Mike, of course, was interested in the list. When he brought the news to Noemi, she felt again, that Mike only wanted to listen to his family. But it dawned on her that perhaps there was a middle truth here. She reasoned that she had only chosen an obstetrician because he was nearby, and perhaps that doctor was not ideal. Perhaps she and Mike could do some research, and that led to her being open to Mike talking to an obstetrician friend who had a number of great recommendations. The issue stopped being black and white. She realized that her own family patterns were feeding into the feeling of not being respected and heard, when perhaps that wasn't the issue at all.

And on all occasions the baby chimed in. One week after Noemi had indeed been having trouble eating, the baby said, "I love you mom, but I need food!" That was all Noemi needed to hear to get her eating pattern in order!

Sometimes I would see them together, sometimes just Noemi, sometimes just Mike. For Mike the themes of guilt and anxiety were the main ones that kept emerging, and as he said to me after one session, "I have guilt of being." His mother and brother, Mike told me, also suffer from great guilt. However, Mike was presently being showered with gifts! Not only was he about to find out that his wife was pregnant, but they had found the house of their dreams and he had just been offered a job as a family doctor in Austria. As he explained to me, the salary he was offered in Austria was much higher for fewer hours of work than he had presently. And the house they were planning to buy was near the Austrian border! He told them he was very much interested, but first wanted to learn German. All these good things happening at once triggered anxiety and sleepless nights. His mind churned. Would he be able to pay for the house? Would he be a good father? And of course, as the sleepless nights increased, the fear that maybe he was just like his grandfather, a true source of panic, came out front-and-center. His mother always reminded him how like his grandfather he was! His grandfather's most salient attribute was his anxiety, so debilitating that it affected his ability to work and in the long run his career.

We used many *DreamBirth* exercises to help, including one allowing Mike to talk to his grandfather ("To call a soul that has passed"), releasing him from wherever in Mike's body and mind his grandfather resided. We did one of his and my favorite exercises, "Reversing the past," where Mike "reversed" all the instances he could remember where he experienced anxiety, and more precisely, not being good enough, as both those feelings seemed to be inextricably connected. The end of the "Reversing the Past" exercise includes taking a peek at the future, where Mike saw himself in his new home with Noemi and the baby.

At that point we connected with the baby, who responded, "I'm looking forward to meeting you too!"

A crisis occurred when they found out the sex of the baby. Both Mike and Noemi were shocked when they found out it was a boy; both of them had been sure it was a girl. I saw Noemi the week they found out. I suggested she go into the womb and talk to the baby, and Noemi apologized for being shocked. It was just that she had been so sure it was a girl!

The baby had an interesting response: He told her he knew his sister. They have always been brother and sister.

I remembered Noemi's first vision: that the girl was in a second-tier cloud! The baby said that his sister kept jumping all over the place and visits the garden also. Perhaps that is why she thought it was a girl! And perhaps a girl is next, the one in the second tier!

Noemi experienced a crisis of faith. Why had her intuition been so wrong? Could she ever trust it? She was starting to worry a lot: was she being harmful to the baby by being around children who often got sick in Kindergarten? Maybe she should not be working as much. Her worrying was beginning to remind her of her mother's worrying. That thought worried her further! To calm the waters, I suggested she go inside and connect with her child and ask him if he had a message.

He did, and this time it was for both of them: He assured them he was in good health, and more importantly, he wanted Mike to love him as if he were a girl!

As Mike's and Noemi's fears and anxieties had not completely abated, it occurred to me, on one of our sessions with both of them together, that perhaps the fears and anxieties had a message.

Talking to an emotion: chair-to-chair

When the figure was asked how she could get rid of the fear,
the answer was quite precise:
"Turn your focus from out to in, and do things that are good for you,
that you enjoy, like reading books, and relaxing."
And from the baby in the womb,
"Oh mommy, you are the most beautiful for me!"
Yet another gift for Noemi!

I was inspired by one of my daughters, who used to write in a college online magazine personal essays where sometimes she addressed her feelings as if they had a consciousness. And realized I could use her idea in a 'chair' exercise I had just heard about in a perinatal lecture, where you play both sides of a conversation by physically changing places, in physical chairs. You can have a conversation between your mother and yourself, your partner and yourself and so on. In one chair you talk as yourself, in the other chair you talk as the other person. It seemed to me that we could easily use an imaginal *DreamBirth* exercise, "Speaking to another's Higher Self" where you have two chairs as well, and in this particular exercise, your higher self talks to another's higher self. I decided to use that exercise and have both Mike and Noemi address the emotion that was most troublesome. For both it was fear and anxiety.

I suggested that they talk to their fear/anxiety, and ask what its purpose was, and if a bargain could be made with it.

Noemi saw her fear as the figure of death, the grim reaper. When she addressed it, it told her he was testing her. When Noemi inquired why was he testing her, and why now, it answered:

> "I want you to get stronger. I am doing it now because you are most vulnerable, it will do you the most good to get stronger now."

He also told her that he tested her 5 years ago.

When the figure was asked how she could get rid of it, of the fear, the answer was quite precise: "Turn your focus from out to in, and do things that are good for you, that you enjoy, like reading books, and relaxing."

Noemi agreed with the advice.

Mike's anxiety also had a specific message:

First, the anxiety told him that it was here to teach him strength and gentleness. Secondly, it told him that he had to accept the anxiety, instead of running away from it. The anxiety finally told him it was not going to be around much longer. His anxiety was right; it was over quite soon after that session.

Noemi got the message several times that she needed to go inside for that feeling of safety and home. She had never got that message as strongly as she did with

"The castle" exercise. The exercise is designed to retrieve parts of oneself that have been thrown away, or imprisoned, hidden in our deepest recesses, relegated, as it were, to dungeons. Noemi's dreaming-self used the exercise quite creatively. The little creature that she saved from the deepest dungeon turned into a princess that wanted to show Noemi her true family. And so, she followed the princess into the forest until the princess finally stopped and sat by a tree.

> "So where is the family?" Noemi asked. The response was clear, and she replied, "The family is inside me."

As Noemi became one with her forgotten self, one with the imaginative loving self that lived inside the tree (inside herself), she was surprised to find that although she was alone in the forest she did not feel alone.

A month after the baby's birth, Mike and Noemi asked me to help with their baby's crying. The crying, of course, made them nervous, which elicited more crying! I connected with the soul of their son, and I was shown two pictures: Mike and Noemi enjoying and relaxing in nature, and then I was taken to the image of the tree in the forest that Noemi had seen in "The castle" exercise, and heard the words, "She needs to go to her inside family."

The love the baby expressed for both his parents came up almost any time we connected with him. As soon as Noemi did an exercise, "Looking at important males in your life" where she connected with the gifts she had received from all the men she had ever known in her life, she said that it felt like Christmas. She had many presents, and she felt festive. We went in to check with the baby. He would be, after all, another male in her life! We asked what he thought about the exercise.

> "Oh mommy, you are the most beautiful for me!" Yet another gift for Noemi!

Whatever fears Mike harbored about having a boy had completely evaporated. He sent me a picture when Sebastian was just about a week old. Mike is holding him, looking at his son's face, with the caption, "I can't believe I am SO in love with this child."

The love continues to grow!

Lynn

*The baby definitely piped in, especially during the first time
we did the garden exercise.
"I want little lizards in the garden, and I want you to know
that I have angels too."*

I first saw Lynn during the pregnancy and birth of her first daughter. I saw her again four years later to help her deal with a miscarriage, and then for the pregnancy and birth of her second daughter. What made working with Lynn unique is that, whenever she was doing a *DreamBirth* exercise or whenever she was on my massage table receiving body work, if a question was asked of the baby, or of her in general, she would dip into a different state and voice, and speak for the child or for whichever ancestor or entity who wished to chime in. It was often difficult to take notes as I had my hands behind her head, or under her sacrum, when the talking would take over. Sometimes, with her permission, I recorded the sessions, and I noted that there were instances when I needed clarifications as to who was talking, and when the voice would address me specifically, I felt free to ask questions.

My notes on her first pregnancy were scant, as it had not occurred to me to tape-record her. I knew she had done shamanic journeying, and I remember always feeling intrigued and awed by what her voice, or those speaking through her would say.

The baby definitely piped in, especially during the first time we did the garden exercise. She wanted little lizards in the garden, but more importantly wanted us to know that, "I have angels too."

Even in the womb, her first daughter was exhibiting an interest in all things of the spirit, as she does now in this life. In a second visit to the garden the baby wanted, "more praying, white animals and a white watch dog." When Lynn did "The chalice" exercise, she was at first nervous that all the colors of the chalice had turned to white, as it reminded her of death. In "The chalice" exercise you imagine a chalice filled to the brim with precious stones of every color, and you let the color of the stones create an aura of the colors around you and the baby. It is done to promote protection and optimism.

When we asked why it was that Lynn was seeing a lot of white light emanating from the chalice, Lynn was told that the white light helped her baby "ground."

Lynn's protectors and ancestors seemed to pipe in through many of the *DreamBirth* exercises. They used every opportunity they had! Lynn saw animals come into the garden for her first pregnancy, and also for her second. A large lioness entered one of her gardens and then a huge Mother Bear. They are there to help her, she was told. She was told as well to let go of all past sadness!

Miscarriage

"It's to wake you up," the soul said, and then added,
"A second baby is coming.
Will you give me a chance to be someone else? I want to keep myself in the
spirit world. I don't want to be upsetting to you all the time. I don't want
to be the dead baby. I want to be a spirit guide; I want to help you."

Four years after the birth of her daughter, Lynn came to see me, very distraught. She had just miscarried a baby. At 10 weeks, they could no longer hear the heartbeat. At first, she tried miscarrying at home like the doctors recommended, but then began hemorrhaging and needed an emergency D&C.

When she came to see me, she was in shock and also suffering guilt, as the pregnancy was a surprise and while she wanted the baby, she feared she wasn't ready.

We connected with the soul that had left.

> "It's to wake you up," the soul said, and then added, "A second baby is coming." And then the voice addressed me! "She needs to do more work," it told me. When I asked for clarification as to what kind of work, the voice said, "Some bodywork and some emotional work."

The voice continued communicating with me. It told me Lynn needed to clear some things with "bad men." The #MeToo movement that coincided with her miscarriage had reopened wounds from past rapes. The child-to-be said these men needed to be taken out of her body. She was told that this experience of clearing, if she were willing do the emotional work that needs to be done, would be a "passport to a major life change." The soul joked that not only would she be given a passport, she'd be given carry-on luggage to a new life!

Lynn responded that she was willing to do the emotional work that needed to be done. "I was afraid to say I wasn't ready, but I wasn't. I now will be!" Lynn meant that she was very ready and wanted to get pregnant. And so, a three-way conversation ensued: the voice of the miscarried soul, Lynn's voice, as her conscious self, and myself.

I asked for some direction. Which part of her body did I need to work on? The voice clearly told me to work on her lower body, and that it was emotionally charged, it added. It told us that the lower body, for Lynn, is connected to the breath and the lungs (Lynn was recently diagnosed with asthma), and also to her mind.

As I moved my hands to her lower body, Lynn described what she was seeing and hearing. She was being told that they were working with her mind and around her mind. After all, she was told, she was a writer, and her voices told her not to worry about it, not to doubt it.

And then she reported being given a wristwatch.

> "A wristwatch?" I asked.

> "Yes, an imaginal wrist watch. It is gold. It is 9 o'clock now. They are showing me that at noon it will be time. I have between now and Christmas to work, at Christmas it will be time." Lynn saw that she would be in Hawaii when the wristwatch would be at midnight.

As Lynn's work schedule pressed, I did not see her again for several weeks. At our next session, in November, we did several conception exercises. The soul of the child that was coming in told Lynn, "to please keep her in her heart as a white light."

Taking rapists out of the body

Imagery as it is done in this work is the way to move the inside!

The work involved several layers and sessions. Not only did we need to take the rapists out of her body, but we first needed to take her father and her mother out as well. Her father was in her feet; he wanted to protect her. He didn't want her to move so fast! Her mother simply did not want to leave, and kept entreating Lynn to be able to stay. "I will leave later," her mother would say. As the exercise "Taking your mother out of your body" directed, Lynn gently but firmly, after imaginally filling her hands and arms with light from the sun, took each one of her parents out. One at a time!

Lynn and I then did several cleansing exercises. One was a very strong exercise called "The tide," where you see all old memories and toxins leave the body, pulled out by a wave, into the depths of the ocean. We then connected with the child to be, the one slated to be conceived, who thanked her for the cleansing work. Lynn exclaimed, "My baby knows I can do this. My baby sees me, my baby who loves me totally." Lynn laughed. "My baby says happiness is opening up. California can happen! Actual happiness can be mine!" Lynn's dream was to move to California and write for a living.

"Why don't you jump into that place in California, see what you see." I suggested. Lynn saw a warehouse where movies are made. She saw a rope and a rainbow. A script she wrote was being made into a movie. Lynn then saw her ancestors appear, cheering her on. They tell her they have been waiting for her to come here. And they hope she will come back and talk more, because they want to keep in touch with her. They seem to be referring to Lynn's ability to communicate with them when she is in a session using *DreamBirth* Imagery and bodywork.

Lynn then added, "My ancestors come to me in my dreams, they see me a lot in my dreams. But they say they know they can come when I am having sessions here, and it's more direct." She is told that many of her ancestors are healers, and that I, (meaning me, Claudia), am a good conduit for them. They tell us that imagery is a way to talk to all other dimensions.

As the soul had predicted, when the watch reached 12, around Christmas, Lynn got pregnant! Both Lynn and her husband were beyond thrilled.

Because of Lynn's ability to speak for the baby, our in-the-womb conversations were more extensive than usual, and in that sense, profound. As the baby that left three months previously, had a strong "boy energy," Lynn assumed it was a boy inside her, but was delighted when she found out it was a girl.

Being a pair, in different dimensions

The baby inside her then showed Lynn, in images,
how connected she was to the whole family.
"I am a pair, a pair with my brother who left.
We are open to each other always. Sometimes we come in together,
and sometimes separately, but we are always connected.
We are beside each other in some way, always."

We went in to talk to the soul. The soul of the baby inside her responded that the boy baby had decided not to come, that he felt he could do more where he was. The soul added that the boy baby would still be around, very much connected to Lynn and to this present child.

The baby inside her then showed Lynn, in images, how connected she was to the whole family. She had known Lynn before and she was so happy to be her daughter. She also had something to say about her sister, "She is a beautiful, highly intelligent, funny girl!"

We did the "Secret garden" again, reminding the baby that this is where she will be born. While in the garden, the baby said she wanted to have Lynn's soul with her. And she wanted to explain to Lynn that she was a pair, a pair with the brother who left. They were open to each other always. Sometimes they come in together, and sometimes separately, but they would always be connected. They would be beside each other in some way, always. The baby also told us that someone else would be with her as well, someone she has known for many lifetimes, and there would also be a pair of angels.

Later, when Lynn felt a lot of activity in her womb and was nervous that the baby wanted to come out, the baby reassured her that she was simply exploring her surroundings, and that it was time for Lynn to get excited now! Two weeks later, she told Lynn that she was starting to think about her descent and her coming out into this world.

> "It is not imminent," Lynn was told, "but it will be sooner than you think. September is my month." It sounded like it would be earlier than Lynn's September 16 due date.

Mountain lions, cougar, mother bear

> *"I'm capable of being many places at once.*
> *I'm coming to understand that when I'm born,*
> *when I'm beside my mother,*
> *I won't be able to do that."*
> —Lynn's second baby

When inviting into the garden all those that were there to support Lynn, the same animals that came into her garden for her first birth appeared. Her garden was like a cave garden, a Hawaiian garden, and there was a waterfall in the cave. "I usually go to that cave," Lynn added.

But a week later her garden changed. When we asked for her support to appear, Lynn said: "I have a mountain lion, it's a mother mountain lion. She's licking my head and there's a bunch of babies. I'm a little scared but she recognizes me."

I suggested she talk to the mountain lion, expressing her slight fear, and to ask the mountain lion why she's there.

> "She's excited for me, she's a cougar actually, and she's coming back, she's collecting me. She's collecting me. She's helping me get ready for the birth, by sensing what I need, and dragging it back to my cave. She keeps telling me to get around less, and to move inside more."

Imagery as it is done in this work is the way to move the inside!

Lynn then saw women from her ancestry approach. Lynn continued: "I am sensing they want me to get out of my structure. They cannot work with me if I am not able to hear them. I have to listen to them, and I don't always want to."

> I suggested that since she was listening right now, what did they most want her to know right now?

> "That they are able to help me, they are capable of hearing me. I don't have to do everything. They can get me anything I need. The bear, from before, will be there, a mother bear. And I can feel her again, she's coaching me from behind, I can feel her around. She has a fresh perspective on what will help, but she can also help my baby come."

Interestingly, the September 16 due date was the exact day of the previous miscarriage.

In a session a few weeks before Lynn's due date, we spent most of the time doing the *DreamBirth* exercises to prepare for labor. (Look at exercises in Chapter 5 of *DreamBirth*.) At the end of the session, we went in to ask the baby if there was anything she wanted to say.

> "Angels are with me. I'm a long-awaited baby. I have a round little face and a beautiful set of limbs."

When asked if she had anything else to say, she offered, "I'm capable of being many places at once. I'm coming to understand that when I'm born, when I'm beside my mother, I won't be able to do that. I have some work to do in my listening, my strength of feeling. I see what I will be in time, with my sense of purpose. I have more than enough white light around me. I have many times felt like I would want to be born to this family. I see myself wrapped in time in soft white light with them, and I pray for them as well, because they will—I see that they think they will be overwhelmed."

And she assured them, "But I'm so fair. I'm a fair baby. I have so much to offer. I hope they understand it will be okay."

"My brother is helping me. He was here this time, he was making the way for me, so you will feel his presence when you are giving birth. He will help you because you got a crash course last year through the miscarriage, and that experience is still with you, and you can use it to open a lot easier and a lot quicker. I hope you understand how much it will prepare you."

The crash course the baby alluded to was Lynn's experience with the miscarriage. It was at the end of this session that Lynn explained what it felt like for her, when her baby, or at times her guides and supporters step in to talk through her. "I feel like I sit back. I literally see myself sitting back on a bench so that they can come through."

And then the baby had more news about the timing of her birth, but even more poignantly about how Lynn's feelings affect her. "I can hold out a little longer, so that you can finish your projects. I want you to see me. I have no option but to be born this month. I will be born this month. I hope you feel good about seeing me. I'm upset. You have been upset. It's my home in your body so I feel what you feel, so feeling good is good for me."

Some of the babies in the womb seem to have a double consciousness and so they can both feel the upset, feel the feelings of the mother, be affected by her hormones and at the same time be able to see the greater picture. They have a bigger vantage point. Important, however, is the gentle reminder the baby gives Lynn that feeling good is good for the baby.

This session involved not only her present baby talking, but also the baby that she miscarried. He explained that he did not want to upset her, as it was his choice to stay in the spirit world. He told her, "Will you give me a chance to be someone else? I want to keep myself in the spirit world. I don't want to be upsetting to you all the time. I don't want to be the dead baby. I want to be a spirit guide; I want to help you." He explained to her that if she could see him in a new way, in a new light, there is much he can help her with.

Lynn asked the spirit guide how she could let go of her pain, "Hold the baby, kiss the baby, and see her open up. I can help her open. It will be exciting to see. That will help you melt the pain away."

And then the spirit guide addressed me again, "Teach her (Lynn) it is okay, acceptable to communicate with us. It's a little strange for people, who are in bodies, but it's not upsetting at all, it's exciting for us. We like it. We want to talk."

In this session, it wasn't just the babies that had something to say. Lynn brought up a problem that she had been having since June, that sometimes her throat felt like it had a thickness, and it felt like sometimes her throat was closing.

I had Lynn look into her throat imaginally, to say what she saw, and to ask her throat what it wanted to say. First Lynn reported what the throat said.

> "It's upset sometimes because it always wants to help me say the right thing. And also, it wants to help me keep from saying anything."

> Lynn described more what she saw and felt about the throat, "I can't always see what is going on in there. It's massive in there. It's a cold place, a feeling of neediness, of needs being unmet, personal needs."

> On a hunch I said to her, "Ask whoever is in your throat to come out. Check who is in the throat?"

Lynn answered, "My sexual assault. I can't think about it right now, but I still want to write about it. I can't quite just say nothing, but I feel like I have to say nothing."

The throat speaks

Now I addressed the throat, "Will this tightness go away once she writes about the sexual assaults?"

The throat's answer was enlightening, "It's okay to open up and talk to people. It's okay to tell things. It's okay to be happy in front of other people. I think you (meaning Lynn), have some issue about not being seen and being able to keep everything inside, so that nobody can attack you or your belongings, or people you love. I have some news. It's okay to open up and breathe into your body, your light, your sense of self. I think you sometimes want me to protect you, but I can't. I can only allow things in and out." The throat's answer gave me great insight into Lynn's fear of being herself, of expressing through her words (in writing and speaking) how she perceived the world. She felt nervous about her extrasensory ability to channel those "from the other side," and that others will not understand or will make fun or exploit her.

The throat was sweetly explaining that it cannot really protect her; the throat's function is to allow things in and out. The throat is the vehicle to let words and thoughts out, and often people feel a throat's constriction when they are not saying what they truly would like to say. The inside logic for Lynn seems to go like this: if I expose who I really am, I, and those I love, may be hurt, and so I better not say all I see, feel and understand. The "throat" or perhaps Lynn's higher self, by way of the throat, is inviting Lynn to be fully herself, inviting her to shine her light, and that all will be safe if she does. And that it is okay to sell the things she writes, and to show her happiness.

Archangel Michael

We went into the ancestral exercise, "Clearing ancestral trauma," to get to the root of the problem of her feeling that it is dangerous to open up and show whom she is. When the cords were cut, as the exercise instructs, Lynn started to laugh. "It's like going to a spa. Archangel Michael is helping me get a haircut and he shows me how many people have been with me lifetime, after lifetime. He says to me, 'It's about seeing each other now. As we are now. And opening our eyes now to what our work is. It's about letting go of the old. All this stuff is over,' he is telling me. 'You have no obligation to your old past. It no longer matters. You have so much to focus on.'" Lynn added, "He is telling me he will release me." Lynn laughed again. "I see myself holding my baby and being happy and not feeling like all these bad things are happening."

I asked Lynn about the souls that were traveling with her. "I see so many. I see hope. We are on a train, celebrating our lifetimes, but most important I can see us going forward. We are going forward together. I see celebration, release. I don't want to go back ever. I have no desire to return."

I asked Lynn if she could peek ahead a bit, ahead in time, what did she see? "I see more people getting free of old ways. I see work to be done in time, with each other. I see emergence of love, of light. I see a loud bang, an enormous explosion, opening up to white light…I lose myself in love with each other. I celebrate myself with each other. I celebrate myself in other people. I don't believe we are still separate."

Perhaps our knowing self, our dreaming self, our Higher Self is one, able to talk through our many parts, so that it can communicate with us, in any way we will listen! I am grateful, however, for Lynn's talent of being able to embody the different entities, and talk for them, so I could hear firsthand. It allows all of us to witness, in more detail, the very knowing and wide consciousness of children before they come in, and in this last session, the knowing, of what may be coming in time, for all of us. A homecoming! A coming into whom we are meant to be: more loving and joyful, compassionate towards all others and ourselves.

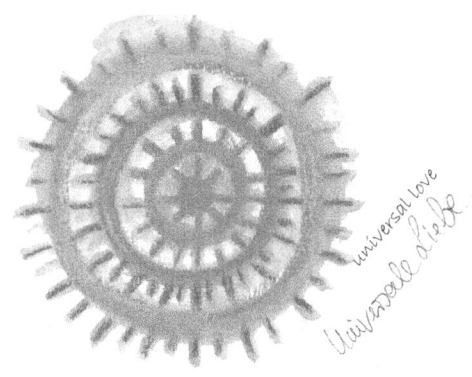

universal love
Universelle Liebe

Chapter 9
Love softens ambition

I used to believe that it was the mothers who searched me out
for a better birth experience.
Now I am more and more of the mind that it is their children
who lead their mothers to me.
It is the babies who want to have a more conscious loving experience.
They want their parents to know that they are lovingly chosen.

Amily's story, on its own, is a Chapter. Her story clearly shows how expectations from one's culture and family affect personal beliefs and attitudes. Because of Amily's talent and ability to do inner work, we are given a full picture of the influences, often not conscious, of how a person is affected by the actions and attitudes of present and past family members. Amily can easily and fluidly dip into past ancestors' lives, and her own past lives. It helps us see how family and ancestral dreamfields weave into the tapestry of the present.

Once I was told by my psychic friend, Patricia, "This ability to do inner work flourishes when life circumstances are particularly harsh, challenging or dry, devoid of life-giving nurturing ideas, beliefs and circumstances." This idea was echoed by a friend from Russia. He firmly believes that Russia's harsh belief systems and totalitarian way of life, has given rise to an attraction to shamans, nature spirits, dream work, and imagery. He believes experience in these more right-brain modalities is what has kept the Russian people more sane and balanced than they otherwise might be.

Every culture, every country, every family has expectations, and unwritten rules about proper behavior and proper attitudes. These expectations are replete with many, many examples of those who follow the expected path. For the last three years I have worked privately with many women from China. Especially for women, what emerges in the imagery, is that the societal expectations in China, are quite harsh and rigid. They do not hold in high esteem independence or following one's own star. This contrasts with the belief in many western cultures, especially in the United States, where independence and 'doing your own thing' are highly valued.

> "In China," according to Amily, "not only is independence and 'doing your own thing' frowned upon, but traditionally girls themselves are not held in high esteem."

Throughout its history, China was known for infanticide of baby girls, and even in the world of adoption, it is the girls that were put up for adoption. During the one-child policy, their prominent belief was, if you can only have one child it was better to have a boy because he would be the one to take care of the parents in their old age. That was the expectation and custom.

The belief in suffering

As Amily put it in one of our sessions, "China believes in suffering." The idea of suffering for the good of the family or for the good of society is seamlessly incorporated into the country's dreamfield. There is a great emphasis on working hard: at school, at work, and at the expense of individual needs. Many of the women I worked with reported being taken care of by grandparents, not always warmly, while the parents worked long hours.

Perhaps because the population is so large, fierce competition is a prevalent reality. At least in the recent historical past, not many receive physically demonstrative, cuddly mothering—there is no time, and no true value placed on it. As a mother or grandmother, your job is to make sure your child succeeds in society. Most of my clients from that part of the world report feeling lonely when they were very young. They yearned to be held and hugged more than they were. When loving touch and attention is scarce, the next source of positive attention is doing very well at school and later work. The thinking is, "If I do very well in school, I will get positive attention from my grandparents and my parents." Ambition to do very well, and earn the positive attention all living beings need to flourish, may be one of the natural outcomes of the Chinese set of beliefs and expectations.

Now we can get to Amily's story.

Amily

"I was holding my baby the other day and trying to put him to bed. He was crawling on my shoulder with some music in the background. For the first time in my 42 years, in this lifetime, I felt it was worth coming to this life."

Amily came to me for help with conception. Amily is very direct, says exactly what she wants, and has a great sense of humor. She interrupted our work for a year at a time, twice. I was beginning to think Amily's inside was not sure she wanted a child, and perhaps had not quite come to terms with that. To be clear, I always leave room to be wrong! It was true she interrupted the work, and it was also true she came back to do the work. And to be clear, many women get pregnant without *DreamBirth*. Amily, however had not, and she had a clear sense that *DreamBirth* would help uncover and clear what lay underneath her inability to conceive.

Amily is a very accomplished businesswoman. She was used to getting whatever she set her mind to, and in interpersonal relations used to getting her way. She worked in the finance industry and commanded a salary in the millions. She was born and raised in China. Her parents were of humble origins, especially her mother's family. Amily had attended a prestigious college in the United States where she got an MBA. She worked in New York City for a number of years, but when she reached out to me, she had moved back to China, and had gotten married. Amily's communications with me, offer the best presentation of whom Amily is, and will make her story easier to tell.

This is Amily's first communication:

> *Hi Claudia,*
>
> *My name is Amily and I heard about you and your work from Lucia. I was wondering whether I could have a few sessions with you. We have been trying to have a baby but it has not gone well...*
>
> *I was wondering whether you could help me?*
>
> *Sincerely,*
>
> *Amily*

During our first session, I learned that Amily was 40-years-old and had gotten married two years before. It was a second marriage for both. Recently she had started to open up to spirit, as she put it. This was new for Amily.

In that first session we did the "Secret garden" both to create a safe space in nature, and to connect with the soul of the baby who was planning to come to Amily. Very interestingly the gate to the garden had two stones in front of it. The stones were there so she could kneel, Amily said. Her inside seemed to know it was a place of reverence! Her garden was full of pink and yellow roses and had a big palm tree. The roses grew wildly.

"I see a little boy come into the garden." She said.

When she asked if he liked the garden, "He smiles. He wants a pool with a slide." In her mind's eye, Amily designed a pool and slide and created, as well, a pink bridge of light from her heart to his to strengthen the communication and connection.

As part of her new inward journey, Amily had also started taking a Course in Light, with Antoinette Moltzan, who considers herself a channel to divine inner knowledge. As Amily put it, that course opened a new door, a new way of perceiving, perhaps a new world. *DreamBirth* fit into that world. Before the pregnancy and the course, all Amily cared about was success in money. As a child she had pushed herself to get very high marks in school. Indeed, three months before this first session, Amily had quit a job in a think tank company where she commanded a very high salary, in millions in US dollars.

Soon after that first session I received four emails. This first one expands on her relationship to money:

> *Hi Claudia,*
>
> *It was a wonderful session yesterday, thank you. When I told you that I am very sure about my decision of walking away from a lot of money yesterday, I heard a voice in my heart saying, "Is it possible because you don't think you deserve it, or because you are afraid of it?"*
>
> *I have to confess that I have very complex feelings about money. On one side, I love money (who doesn't?) because it provides a good quality of life and freedom for me and my family; on the other side, being in the financial service industry for over 10 years both in the U.S. and especially in China, I've seen too many people making money in immoral ways (so I remind myself all the time that I don't want to be them; I want to make clean money).*
>
> *On top of that, my parents are very humble people (especially my mom; so humble that she always questions my ability and my achievements). I am the youngest translator publishing two books from Japanese to Chinese in China at age 23; I earned a full scholarship to finish my MBA and then became the first person in my school landing a job on Wall Street; I built a business making 30–40 million dollars for my company; (but she thinks it's pure luck and always reminds me to stay low profile so that I am not running out of luck).*

> *I don't think it's because she doesn't love me. Instead, I think it's because she doesn't have confidence in herself and she feels insecure. But her beliefs seem to be rooted in me, so that I believe I am not worth that much money that it was luck and I have to run away before it collapses. (Of course, from my professional understanding, it won't last long either; but I don't know out of the two thoughts, which affects which).*

Later that same day she sent the following communication:

> *Hi Claudia, funny thing is when I think about the letter I sent to you this morning, I hear myself saying "I love money, I will make more money, but I will quit my previous job twice" not sure what impacts me so much there (in previous job, that is) :)*
>
> *So, maybe we can address these in our later sessions? Thank you.*

At least in the beginning, she could not come up with a single reason why having a baby was good.

Very quickly after that email, the plot thickened and she sent me this fourth one:

> *I've also listed thoughts on my mind when I think about baby. Funny that nothing positive came.*
>
> *- Lifetime concerns*
> *- Potential risk that baby doesn't develop well*
> *- No personal time any more*
> *- Big body size for a long time*
> *- Sleepless nights*
> *- No tidy house for a long time*
> *- Endless noise*
> *- Money*

When we met for our next session the issue of control is what was most salient, and what she wanted to work on. Her husband was now in the mix. He chimed in when he heard that control issues were something Amalie wanted to work on:

indeed, he felt she was controlling. Amily's attitudes towards other people, and her wanting to have her way became a running theme in our sessions.

She mentioned as well that the company she had just left 3 months ago wanted her back. They were willing to take her back as a consultant or full-time employee. "We need you," was the message they communicated. She was tempted as the salary was very generous, but she was not sure she wanted to go back. In her estimation, she and the company held different moral standards. Her question to me was whether she should go back. The money was tempting.

To get an answer, I taught her the "The feather of truth" imagery exercise as well as another way, to get a "yes" or "no" from her body, using a form of muscle testing.[20] Using imagery or her actual body was a way that Amily could mine her deeper knowledge. It is one of the ways to connect to a greater knowing we all seem to possess, not one embedded in the conditioning of our culture, our family and our interpretation of life events. Imagery taps into this greater knowledge, and the body itself, directly, can also reveal the greater truth, which is always more life-giving and love filled than any other 'truth.' It is through our body's knowing that we often know something is not right. We may feel a tightening in our gut, or a quickening of the heart. The body 'knows it' before our mind or consciousness has registered that something is amiss. The fact that Amily had heard she would leave the company twice intrigued me. Amily could not leave the company twice if she did not go back a second time! What interested me was that she could 'hear' or sense her intuitive knowing.

We talked as well in this session about contracts one makes before coming in, or after one is born, and that these contracts can be changed. One is allowed to change one's mind! Perhaps there was a different way for Amily to learn that it is not the most optimal way of life, to insist or to force her 'own way.'

We used the strongest exercise we have to get to the source of her control issues: the "Clearing ancestral trauma" exercise mentioned in Noemi's and Patricia's story. As I suspected, especially working with women from China, the source often is not only in the family/ancestral dreamfield, but often in past lives and in

---

[20] See Dr. Bradley's *The Emotion Code*. Mesquite, Nevada: Wellness Unmasked Publishing, 2007.

the history of China itself as well. The family/ancestral dreamfield is very much shaped by the beliefs and traditions of the greater culture. Even though Amily is very logical and business-oriented she had no trouble dipping into her dreaming knowledge—she could easily, during an imagery exercise, access knowledge and feelings of past lives, or those of her ancestors.

Needing to be Number One

The dreamfield gets passed on to future generations.
It is part of the web of memories, thoughts and feelings
that get passed on from mother to baby,
whether the mother is aware of it or not.

Throughout our sessions we needed to do the ancestral exercise several times, and the issues we worked on seemed to be connected: fear of failure, needing to be "Number One," fear of poverty and needing to feel better than others. Each time a different layer of the onion, a different aspect of the problem would be revealed. The first time we did the exercise several memories emerged. The first layer that emerged was fear of being wrong, with the added twist of needing to be Number One. The exercise has you go quickly back through your life, noting the first time the problem at hand first materialized, and in Amily's case, to remember the very first time Amily experienced the fear of being wrong. Very quickly she came to a memory of herself in first grade, being very afraid she would get a wrong answer, and not get a 100. She got the highest grade in the class, but it was a 99.

"What happened when you were not Number One?" I asked.

Amily's paternal grandmother entered the picture. It was not good to get any wrong. It was dangerous to get any wrong. I intuited there was more to this fear. The exercise next asks to go back to the womb, and sense if there was anything in the womb that reflected this energy.

"In my mother's womb I feel sad."

A string of memories of being sad, memories of yearning to be hugged by her mother, memories of her mother not spending time with her, flooded her consciousness. "I also feel my mother's sadness while I'm in the womb, not just mine. I know she was not happy. She believed she deserved somebody other than my father."

It was clear that Amily's issue of being better than someone was embedded in that memory, and created the need to be Number One, and to be contemptuous of anyone who was not Number One.

As one works this exercise, first tuning into the feelings in the womb, then tuning into the felt experience at one's own conception, going back further, to look at the decision one made to come into the world to these parents. After that, the exercise asks one to zero in as to what one's mission for this life is.

In the exercise, when Amily was asked what her mission for this life was, she saw two words: "love and relationship." Amily saw that needing to be Number One came from her mother's dreamfield—the mother's experiences and thinking.

> "I see my mother when my mother was a little girl, around 5-years-old. My mother's father is in the hospital, and my mother's mother goes to take care of him. I see my mother, around 5-years-old, feels helpless and lost. She did not know where her mother had gone. I see her going out to look for her. It's raining, and a neighbor finds her forlorn."

Apparently before her father got sick, they lived a good life, with some affluence. After the father's illness the family struggled to make ends meet.

Amily's mother stayed strongly with the feeling that she loved her mother and missed her father. She was not hugged or paid attention to. Amily's mother did not learn how to hug. As Amily opened her eyes, Amily said to me, "My mother did not hug me because she didn't know how."

The origin of her need to be Number One did not seem to have been answered. Her dreaming self, her knowing self, had brought up the issue we perhaps needed to work on first. I have learned to very much trust information her higher self was providing and could see that not being hugged as a baby and small child was an important issue to deal with.

However, Amily herself noted that the question of being Number One had not really been addressed. Amily volunteered that it came from her paternal grandmother who always told her to "Be Number One." Amily's dreaming self easily accessed the origin of this thinking, and so we continued the exercise. We asked to see the origin of this idea.

Amily was shown the following scene. She saw people on horses, running. One of the horses she saw was running away from a battle. She saw mainly men. From the men's clothing it looked like the battle happened around 300 years ago, perhaps more. The ancestor in this scene was a farmer. He lived a very normal life. There seemed to be a war between two nations.

The exercise then asks the subject to look at what was happening before the traumatic event, and then to go to the end of this person's life, to tune into the thoughts and feelings of that person at the time of death. Those feelings and thoughts are strong, and they are therefore imprinted strongly in the family dreamfield. This ancestor died in the scene Amily witnessed, and his feelings at death were:

"You have to be faster and stronger, next time."

Remembering the life-giving aspects of a memory

That experience, that emotion and the corresponding belief affects everyone connected to this ancestor. It becomes an integral part of this family's dreamfield, their web of feelings and experiences. The dreamfield gets passed on to future generations. It is part of the web of memories, thoughts and feelings that get passed on from mother to baby, whether the mother is aware of it or not. As we have mentioned before, the baby's feelings are in the same soup as the mother's. That is not to say that wonderful qualities, beliefs, and memories are also present in the family dreamfield. Many of us are imbued with memories and beliefs of perseverance, courage, love, and many other life-giving beliefs. Those wonderfully affect us. It is the beliefs and memories that are not life-giving that we need to uncover and transform. Or simply and gently release them. That is why this exercise is so helpful. Often seeing them in the light of consciousness automatically transforms them, or lets one release them. They are truly not relevant anymore.

The next few sessions dealt with whether Amily should accept one of the jobs that she was being offered; unfortunately, anger towards her husband, was strongly emerging. Discord with a partner often affects conception. Her first complaint was that he did no housework whatsoever, and he didn't clean up any of his messes. Her husband told her he genuinely did not see the mess. He told her he was fine with her telling him to clean up. The real problem was that Amily did not believe him. She told me that she only trusted three people: her mother, her father, and one of her girlfriends.

Amily was also angry at her husband because of money. She felt she was the one that was bearing the brunt of their expenses. Her husband had made a bad investment a few months before they got together where he lost around 2 million dollars. And although he currently made a good salary, he was mainly paying back that poor investment. He planned to be out of that financial hole in six months to a year, but again, Amily did not believe him. She had paid for their car and their house. She was feeling put upon by and contemptuous of him.

Amily then admitted that the feeling of contempt was not new for her; she had also been contemptuous of her first husband. He was from the United States, and a very devoted and loving husband, but he made much less money than she did. Her contempt, she told me, was quite tied to her mother's attitude of contempt for men in general. Amily felt that her mother had planted the seed of contempt for her present husband. Her mother, Amily told me, was very judgmental. The mother felt that Amily and her present husband came from very different backgrounds. Amily had traveled a lot more, had seen more of life, and that their views would then necessarily be very different. Amily's mother was also concerned that money would get in the way, and that Amily should always have control of her money and possessions; it was safer that way.

Working on her attitude and relationship to men

The baby encouraged her,
"Harmonize your relationship with my father.
It is not complicated."

I understood that we needed to work on her attitude and relationship to her husband, and men in general. There are two exercises in *DreamBirth* that I often go to when there is a problem in a relationship. The first one, "Return to a place of love" is asking the person to remember in felt, vivid detail the first time they realized this person was the right person for them. The second one is to stand in the shoes, in the body (imaginally) of the other person. This exercise, "Stepping into someone's shoes" truly helps to feel/sense from the other person's perspective.

When I asked Amily to experience the day, the time she knew her husband was the right person for her; she reconnected with those thoughts and feelings.

The good feelings were varied: He was cute, he had investments, he was funny, he was smart, and he had long legs. His personality was cheerful. She had used an expensive matchmaking company that had given her 7-to-8 candidates. The company used the men's birthday as part of the criteria. Her husband was number two. At least at this point in her thinking, there was no consciousness that a relationship can be more than transactional, that it can provide the more intangible pleasures—of acceptance, companionship, support and love. These were attributes she had not learned at home.

The very first time Amily experienced contempt for her husband provided a perfect opportunity, a real opening, for her to go imaginally into her husband's body and experience things from his point of view. The first time she felt contempt for her husband was early on in their dating. He had brought bread to have at a dinner at her place. What bothered her, and engendered contempt, was that he took a piece of bread first, and then he took home the leftover bread. When she entered his body in that particular situation she saw that he felt innocent, that Amily had strict standards, and that he was powerless.

I changed tactics. I asked Amily when was the first time she felt judged. Often, if one judges another harshly, there will be the experience of having been judged harshly oneself. In this case, for Amily, it was during primary school. She was a big kid, somewhat fat, and she felt her peers judged her. She volunteered that contempt was necessary; she needed to feel better than others. When I asked her why that was necessary, she told me because she needed to be seen, to be important.

Amily confessed that she was in the process of cleaning out her closets, and that she wanted to kick out all of her husband's clothes. Ahh, more work needed to be done!

When we met next, I asked if anything had changed in the way she related to her husband. When she saw him now, she told me, she saw him as a 7 or 8-year-old boy. He was very happy because she did everything for him. Not only did she contribute most of the money but when she thought about them having a child, she saw herself as having to provide the money, do the housework and do the childcare. Traditionally Chinese men never help with the housework. Additionally, his parents spoiled him, Amily felt. As a child, they never let him do anything, not even help clear the table or even bring dishes to the table. Amily's husband's solution was to hire a cleaning lady. That way Amily would have help. Amily told me her mother had warned her that he would use money to solve everything. There was a lot of resentment here!

To sit at the feet of God: Higher Self to Higher Self

It is the listening to the other that often makes a difference.

I suggested having a talk with her husband—Higher Self to Higher Self. I reminded her that her Higher Self had been with her every lifetime, and his Higher Self also was very wise. And besides, I told her, all Higher Selves are in communication with each other. The exercise, "Speaking to another's Higher Self," has each person sit on a chair, and the chairs go up as high as they need to, so that they are truly talking to each other from their higher selves. If they report to me the same old arguments, I tell them to go higher, to go as high as is needed to truly communicate Higher Self to Higher Self. It is fascinating to me that when that is done, the tenor of the conversation changes. I have had a few clients tell me they had to go as high as God, to sit at the feet of God to finally talk and listen through their Higher Self. If they are not religious, they go up as high as the stars. The exercise asks that the conversation continue, until there is a resolution. Some clients want to stop after they have told the other all they wish. I insist they continue, and listen to what the other's response is, and then to respond to that. It is the listening to the other that often makes a difference.

Amily told her husband of her concerns. He responded that it would not always be that way. Once his debt was paid off he, would be able to contribute to their household expenses. Furthermore, he told her, they could solve the housework in a different way. He was not going to change his ways in that regard, but he would provide help. He would love to spend time with their child. He especially would do that when the child was a little older, he told her. They are talking, of course, about the child not yet conceived!

Amily, however, as before, did not believe him. She told me they had had a very explosive fight, that week, but that he stood his ground. I could see this was a very new experience for Amily. She was used to a partner completely giving in to her. The fight was about her going to a house they have at the south end of China. She wanted to go and spend two or three months there, by herself. He told her that if she went, he would invite his parents to come and stay at their present place. She realized that it was not a crazy request. Part of her was happy that he stood up for himself.

It was time to bring in their child to be! She connected with him in the garden and the child said he was happy with the work she was starting to do. We connected as well with her ancestral support, which she saw as a large crowd. They told her that she was starting to do a lot of work to explore herself, but that she had just entered the door. "Keep doing what you are doing," they advised.

A wrinkle emerged in the situation. Her husband had his sperm checked, and according to the results, less than 5% qualified as good, healthy sperm. The doctors advised that he do a lot more exercise, especially lifting, and that he needed to sleep more each night. She understood that they would have to wait until his sperm got 'in better shape.' We went in again to talk to the spirit of the child that was planning to come in. This time she saw him as a five-year-old boy, at the beach. She saw him running towards her. He told her he felt lonely but that he could wait two to three months. "Communicate with me every day," he admonished.

In this session Amily again did the exercise to enter the body of her husband. There was a change. This time she could see how he loved her, and it was the first time, she told me that she could see he had a soul!

We tuned into the baby again, and this is what the baby said: "I am excited about coming in." He said as well that his plans were to teach them how to love. He told her not to be anxious and to be patient. Things would happen. The soul also told Amily to not skip physical exercise. He told his father to drink more water and to do exercise every day. Then Amily saw the baby clap his hands and laugh. She saw that he laughed like his father. He came into their dreams, he said, just to say, "Hi."

A few weeks later, the sperm were tested again, and they had improved. Even so, Amily felt that the improvement was not enough, and they decided to do a round of IUI[21] to maximize the effectiveness of the sperm. We went into the garden again to connect with the soul. The baby encouraged her, "Harmonize your relationship with my father. It is not complicated." He preferred that the event be more pleasurable and happier. The soul had more advice about their relationship. "Both of you have your own perspective on things." He told them that part of learning how to love was to understand a different perspective.

He also told Amily that she had a lot of unnecessary worries. She need not worry that having a job would be harmful. And most of all, the soul added, she need not worry that his father won't be a good Dad. "He will spend a lot of time with me." But the soul added that the father would not change his attitude about housework. "His father's parents spoiled him," the soul concurred.

---

[21] Intrauterine insemination (IUI)—a type of artificial insemination—is a procedure for treating infertility. Sperm that have been washed and concentrated are placed directly in your uterus around the time your ovary releases one or more eggs to be fertilized.

The soul wanted to be thought about more. The soul told Amily that his father would give Amily the gift of a new perspective on how to live a happy life. The father would gift Amily with a more positive attitude, a sense of humor and companionship. Amily was teaching the father about spiritual enlightenment and how she managed relationships with people. The baby advised the mother to be more positive, patient, and more accepting of the father.

I then gave Amily the "Take three steps back" exercise, as it often engenders more compassion. After taking some steps back, imaginally, from her husband, Amily was able to see that he allowed her to be successful. In fact, he showed her off to others about those successes, and the amount of money she spent on spiritual endeavors. She could see that he adored her. This was a change.

Very soon after that session she got a job offer from where she used to work, but before accepting it she negotiated a 60% increase over the salary being offered. She would need to be in the office, 9:00–6:00, 5 days a week to build up a new team. She would only see her husband on weekends. She knew, however, that this job would be temporary.

She also had given a lot of thought to the relationship with her husband. She realized how 'heart breaking' she could be toward her husband, not really taking his feelings into account. She had changed a lot of her attitudes, she reported. She had had the past life awareness that she had been a general, the head of a tribe in one lifetime, and 'saw' that her husband was the general's bodyguard.

She indeed was learning to accept her husband more. Their future child had more to add to this conversation. It would be good to add that having a baby can be a fun journey, the baby said, "And don't take it as a long journey." She could relax and believe her son would come.

Amily took a break from sessions with me while she went to work. A year-long break! They did try a few sessions of IUI, which were unsuccessful. Amily returned to have sessions a year later. Amily reported that they planned to do a few more IUI's because the sperm were still not active enough. She had done an IUI procedure 10 days prior. She did not get pregnant.

However, Amily was now having a new set of thoughts, a real change of heart. She reported that she now did not want to have a child. This new thinking began with a conversation she had had with her mother. Her mother was now happy that Amily had a normal life especially because Amily now lived near her. Her mother explained she had wanted Amily to have a baby because of the social impact that implied. I am not sure what was meant by that, but it started to free Amily from what she felt was expected of her.

When she presented her thinking to her husband, he suggested that her parents and his parents would step in to help if she needed more time for herself. He assured her they would be happy to. Amily was expecting her husband to say, "It's your choice," and was thrown when her husband expressed a desire for a life with children. The fact that he did not just leave it up to her was making her have some doubts.

I suggested she talk to the soul of the baby, as this very much concerned him. The garden today had different-colored flowers, not just the usual red and pink ones. She called the soul and connected heart to heart, telling the baby of her current thinking: that she did not want to have a child.

She reported that he nodded and smiled and said he still wanted to come, but understood, and that it was all right with him. However, he asked to be held by her, and he jumped into her arms. He told her she still had time to figure it out.

The next session revealed the strength and extent of her husband's reaction.

Limitless love

Her husband passionately wanted to have a child because of 'limitless love.'
A lot of things came to the fore. She told her husband she felt pressed by
society, her parents, her peers. She felt she had no choice.

I asked her if anything had cleared from that talk and her last session. Yes, she said, she felt heard. If it were just up to her, the decision was made, but she was starting to realize it was not just her decision. Her husband had a very strong opinion. As he put it, "I want a baby, I have a part in this! How can I show you that I want to have a baby?" She thought part of his feelings were a result of their age, that this would be their last chance. But he insisted, "I can't imagine my life without a kid."

She admitted to being surprised. She never realized how strongly he wanted to have a child. But she didn't want to have a baby just because he wanted to. I asked her if she was willing to let go of the relationship with her husband if he truly wanted to have children? If they broke up or didn't have children, she said that she would go to India for 21 weeks and attend a yoga teacher training.

The true conundrum emerged. She did not want to be the person who broke up the relationship. She didn't want to fail expectations. The financial situation had also changed. She had just quit her $300,000 a year job, as she felt there was not much to do. (This made true her vision that she would quit her job twice, with the same company!) Her husband had got a new job that paid more, and he was finished paying off his debts. He wanted to buy his parents an apartment. If her investments continued to give her a 10% return, she was fine. She also had several other apartments. All in all, she felt this would be enough financial support for now.

We returned to her persistent feeling that she needed to meet expectations. "I want to be praised," she told me, and that had to do with meeting expectations. I asked her to see when the first time this feeling had occurred, and her dreaming knowledge took her straight to other lifetimes.

Amily saw a little girl, in China, around 100 years ago. It seemed that if the little girl did not do a good job, there would be no food. She saw that the little girl died of starvation, at around 8 or 9-years-old. The little girl felt she had been working hard to earn her food, but she must not have worked hard enough. When the cord was cut, so that the whole family field was not enthralled by this memory, Amily saw that the little girl quickly became an angel. We asked the archangel to cut any invisible cords that tied the ancestry to this type of memory. Amily saw the archangel cut many, many invisible cords. The angel's message to her after all the cutting was, "Your soul is free now. You can pursue what you want.

Archangel

Amily connected with the soul that was planning to come in.
The garden was full of roses of all colors.
"I want to kiss you," the soul said.
I asked Amily how that made her feel in her body.
"I feel love in my heart."

Interestingly Amily and her husband had come upon a compromise. Her husband proposed that they try IUI two more times. "If you don't get pregnant, we don't try anymore." I asked Amily if she was truly okay with this decision. Yes, she told me. She had decided to surrender to the greater will, the greater good for all involved.

Not all was well, however. Amily was gripped with fear that the baby might not be okay, and that there would be something wrong with the baby. She realized what was behind that was the belief that to grow one must suffer. She wanted to work on that belief. And that is what we did the following session.

Right away we went into the origin of that belief. The first scene Amily saw was a battle scene in China, several hundred years ago. There was a lot of killing. The person she was looking at was a man, who looked like he was killing around 30 or 40 people. He lived but was killed later by the enemy. At his deathbed she saw him alone and thinking he should have tried harder and killed more people. Fifty or sixty would have been better, he felt.

Then Amily was shown another life, of either an ancestor or a past life. She was shown a woman around 30-years-old. The woman was washing clothes by a river. She was washing clothes for a family. She felt very unhappy and stuck. Her whole lifetime she worked very hard, and at her death, around 70 or 80-years-old, she was alone. She felt bitter; life was very difficult, nothing was good.

The pictures that were emerging were of suffering, with no respite. Amily told me she felt this was China's belief system—one must pay with pain. This imprint did not just belong to her family dreamfield.

From these stories I didn't see the instances of growth because of adversity. The idea of hurting as a fact of life seemed to be front and center.

Amily called on all the angels that protect, "Please help all those suffering ancestors, and all those suffering in my country." She saw them spreading snowflakes all over China.

The advice of Archangel Michael, this time, was that Amily was free, and that she would learn from her future life that life did not have to be hard, that she was blessed. He told her that her future life would hold much happiness. When Amily poured the transformation water on all her ancestry she saw the ancestry light up. She put the last drop of water on her third eye.

After the exercise Amily connected with the soul that was planning to come in. The garden was full of roses of all colors. The soul wanted to kiss Amily. I asked Amily how that made her feel in her body. "I feel love in my heart," she responded.

I received this email shortly after this last session:

> Hi Claudia,
>
> I am pregnant!! Are you surprised? Yes, 3 days after our last session, we did our second IUI, and I am pregnant!
>
> Amily

Amily Postscript: heart to heart

"I came all this way to find you—how can you say I do not love you!"
—Amily's son

I have continued working on and off with Amily, both during her pregnancy and after the birth of her son. I often remind mothers that they can talk to their children out of the womb like they did while in the womb or like they did before conception. They can talk to the child through the ethers—heart to heart, mind to mind or Higher Self to Higher Self. Amily talks to her child often in this fashion.

Recently, Amily's 5-month-old son has started to say 'Ma.' At this point he practiced it both with the nurse that he has known since birth, and with Amily. During a particularly difficult and overwhelming week for Amily she thought she heard her son say 'Ma' more to his nurse than to her. In a momentary fit of self-pity, she talked to her son, through the ethers, accusing him of loving the nurse more than Amily.

This was her son's response: "I came all this way to find you—how can you say I do not love you!"

A few weeks later I received this short email from Amily:

> *"I was holding my baby the other day and trying to put him to bed. He was crawling on my shoulder with some music in the background. For the first time in my 42 years, in this lifetime, I felt it was worth coming to this life."*

angel

Engel

Chapter 10
The universe of the heart

The more stories I hear of the babies who were born using DreamBirth the more heartened I am about who is coming into this world.

I used to believe that it was the mothers who searched me out for a better birth experience. Now I am more and more of the mind that it is their children, those souls in the womb or those wanting to come in, who find me and lead their mothers to me, (or others who do this work). It is the babies who want to have a more conscious loving experience. They want their parents to know that they are lovingly chosen, that it is not a haphazard arrangement and that they have much to say, especially if they are treated as the fully conscious beings that are present. The more stories I hear of the babies who were born using *DreamBirth* the more heartened I am about who is coming into this world.

Maya, Caterina's child

"I came from the Universe of the Heart."
—said Baby Maya to her God Mother Stephanie

I am a good friend of Stephanie, the God Mother of Caterina's child, Maya. Maya, used to wave and smile at Caterina (Chapter 4), when in the womb. Maya, when she was three-and-a-half, on the day before Stephanie was about to leave for a four-month stay in New York, called her God Mother over to her, and the following conversation ensued:

"Stephanie, I want to tell you where I come from."

"Tell me, Maya, where do you come from?"

"Well, of course I came from my mommy's belly, but I came from somewhere before that."

"Where was that, Maya?"

Maya put her hands on her heart.

"You came from there? From the Heart?"

"Not just my heart, Stephanie. I came from the Universe of the Heart."

And so, they speak like that!

Verification: babies hear the exercises in the womb

Early in our work with Catherine as I was learning *DreamBirth*, one of the doulas in the original training, sent all of us who were part of that training a remarkable email verifying that the babies in the womb do indeed 'listen' to the exercises and are affected by them.

She wrote to us that a young boy, about 5-years-old at the time, whose mother had used *DreamBirth*, was dying. His mother remembered how much she had been helped by the exercises and asked the doula if there was something she could do to help her son. The mother had particularly liked "The Blue Vase Exercise," and so they decided, as the little boy was in a coma-like state, that having his sister read the exercise might be particularly soothing to him. "The Blue Vase Exercise" is a staple in the *Saphire* tradition, and can both energize you and calm you. The exercise instructs you to breathe out—as a light smoke—all that tires you, disturbs you or obscures you, and on the inhalation, you breathe in blue, blue light made golden by the sun. The light you breathe circulates down the back of your body, and then up the front until you become so light filled, you look like a Crystal Vase, filled with light, shining in all directions. And so, they gave the exercise to the sister to read, and as she was 'giving' the exercise, her brother, who had not opened his eyes or talked in many days, opened his eyes and said,

"I remember this, from long, long ago. I remember doing this."

Lori's baby

Another story concerns my client, Lori, who once called me when her daughter was about 6-months-old. Lori had come to me when she was 8 or 10 weeks pregnant, and had come weekly to my office, learning many, many *DreamBirth* exercises. Her daughter had never been inside my office, except, of course, when she was in the womb.

Lori called me in disbelief. "Claudia, I don't know what to make of this. I was going past your building when the baby began to point very excitedly towards your building. I tried to see if there was anything kid-friendly around, like balloons, or a poster, or festive store window decorations, but Claudia, there was nothing. She just kept pointing to your building, to that front entrance, with great excitement."

Galactic Marker

*There has been a noticeable change, as well, in what women see,
when they visualize their ancestral support. When I first began this work
in 2003 most clients could see no more than three or four ancestors, some
perhaps 10, but recently more and more people
see hundreds, or uncountable numbers.*

I am struck with how more and more, since 2012, the year humanity passed the galactic marker,[22] the time period heralded in many indigenous cultures as the time human consciousness will rebalance back to wisdom, love and compassion, that the mothers can see and hear more in the imagery exercises. They also don't question the concept that it is possible to talk to their babies in the womb. Moreover, they easily take in stride that they can talk to their babies before they are conceived, that they can talk to those in their life that have left because of miscarriage, or that they can make amends with those that have been aborted. Even more surprising to me is how much more open the fathers are to this work. They love talking to their unborn children, and very much welcome being able to participate during the birth, using the imagery. They understand, more than they ever did, that what they do through imagery will have powerful effects in their life.

I worked with a father, recently who, when he learned the exercise to imagine all doctors in light, with instruments in light, turned to me, and asked, "Would it be okay if I imagined all people I meet to be in light?" As my teacher Catherine would say, "Bravo!" He has completely understood that doing that will bring out the best in all.

---

[22] December 21, 2012 is the year humanity passed the galactic marker, an astrological event and time period heralded in many indigenous cultures as the time human consciousness will rebalance back to wisdom, love and compassion. The prophesies of this event and the consciousness that will flourish after the marker is passed, are found in the Maya, Inca, Hopi and other indigenous cultures. There is much written about this, but an excellent source is Chapter 3 of *The Women of Lemuria: Ancient Wisdom for Modern Times* by Kryon and Monika Muranti. Outremont Canada: Ariane Books, 2018.

There has been a noticeable change, as well, in what women see, when they visualize their ancestral support. When I first began this work in 2003 most clients could see no more than three or four ancestors, some perhaps 10, but recently more and more people see hundreds, or uncountable numbers. One day when I was feeling uncharacteristically despondent about the work, and truly doubting its efficacy, I decided to see how many beings were supporting me. I was humbled. It looked as though I was surrounded by many, many beings. Hundreds, if not thousands of ancestors, completely filled the park I was strolling through. I have more help doing what I am doing than I could ever, ever in my life envision. It is fun to close my eyes, and simply look inside, with my inner vision, and ask to see the help each person has. Once I did it for Catherine, and what I saw was almost blinding!

I invite you to try it, to see who is there for you. Do it when you are very relaxed, close your eyes gently, breathe out slowly three times, counting backwards from three to one, and ask to be shown. You too may be surprised.

gratitude

Chapter 11
How I received ovaries of light

Through the imagery exercises I learned to talk to my deceased parents through the ethers, like I now teach my clients to talk to their babies in the womb or after a miscarriage or abortion.

A word is in order here; why am I including the story of my bout with cancer in a book about what babies have to say? The answer is quite simple. Through this experience I was privileged to use many of the *DreamBirth* exercises that I taught my clients. I needed to use "The garden to prepare for procedures" to be ready for my eventual operation and chemo treatments, but more importantly many of the exercises cracked open my soul. My creativity emerged through my responses to the imagery exercises, what I 'saw' was a mirror of my inside, and I could see its beauty. Through the imagery exercises I learned to talk to my deceased parents through the ethers, like I now teach my clients to talk to their babies in the womb or after a miscarriage or abortion. The imagery was healing, extraordinary in its effects. I often say that using the imagery for my own life and death ordeal truly showed me its power, and gave me, in effect, a 'PhD' in imagery. Without this experience I never would have been able to elicit the healing and transformation, and sense of awe that many of my clients experience. After using it myself, I knew its power and it was easy to automatically communicate a sense of knowing and belief. However, after seeing the results of many who have trained with me, this is not really necessary, as the imagery works even if you do not believe in it!

My cancer story illustrates vividly the connection between beliefs, their resulting emotions and how they can house themselves in the body; all this I clearly saw in my clients after experiencing them myself. I could then successfully help them navigate the emotional entanglements of mistaken beliefs, and lead them to a more hopeful, loving, and happy mindset.

And I also learned that the universe gifts us in mysterious ways.

My father's illness

I would pour light on my father and the doctors and nurses. Sometimes I would visualize him in nature, while we were in the emergency room. He would say to me, while the lights were very bright overhead, machines buzzing and some patient's wailing and moaning, "It's so peaceful in here." Oh, the power of imaginal light!

In 2003, the year I started to work with Dr. Catherine Shainberg, I spent much of my attention focused on my father, as well as on my new studies to learn imagery for pregnancy and birth. My father had been diagnosed with prostate cancer a few years earlier, and although he had been fighting the cancer fairly well, when he lost most of his eyesight unexpectedly in a routine cataract operation, the story changed.

He had been quite an energetic and youthful man, who possessed a large yet understated sense of humor, peppered with what can only be described as black humor that often sent those around him into embarrassed peals of laughter. He rode a motorcycle until age 75, and only stopped because the bike was stolen. The cataract surgery, which left him legally blind, definitely took a greater toll on him than the cancer. Life was not as much fun for him. Having been a reporter in the heydays of reporting (1950's and 60's) he prided himself with 20-20 vision.

His vision, his curiosity and his sense of adventure had enabled him to interview first-hand and on the ground many of the Latin American revolutionaries of the 50's and 60's. He spent time with Che Guevara in the wilds of Argentina, and covered whatever news came out of Latin America during those decades. He was a *Time* and *Life Magazines* foreign correspondent, responsible for all news from Latin America.

My mother had died many years earlier, and so my father enjoyed the companionship of many beautiful women; beautiful women were indeed his passion. Interestingly, after his cataract surgery he could not see me walking across the room, coming towards him, but he could 'see' any beautiful woman that came anywhere near him. And he could, I must say, describe very accurate details.

Once his mobility and freedom were impaired, and things were not as interesting or fun, his cancer began to metastasize. I decided to work out of his apartment so that I could keep him company the three days that I came into the city to give Alexander Technique or CranioSacral sessions. We transformed one of the bedrooms in his apartment into my studio.

One of the down sides of having adopted so late in life (my first daughter I adopted when I was 48, the second one when I was 50) is that my children were not grown when it was time to start to take care of my elderly father. My children were three and five, and required attention. As childcare was beyond our means at that point in our lives, my husband, a working actor then, would take care of the girls when I was at my father's, when he could. I often had to cancel appointments, or bring the girls to my father's. When I did bring them, ostensibly my father could watch them while I gave sessions. I found that the reality was that my five-year-old daughter was taking care of him! Very sweetly she would take him by the hand and help him get to the bathroom or his bedroom.

My only sister, who lives in Germany, would visit as often as she could, and take over the care of my father. It became clear that he could not really take care of himself, even though he insisted he could, and so we began the task of finding a place where he would not be living on his own. Not so fast! Visiting a very well-known facility with a wonderful reputation, he turned to me and said, "The people here are so old!" He of course, at 87, was older than many of the residents.

As he had no interest in moving, we miraculously found a young, beautiful girl from Russia who needed the work and came every afternoon, rotating the times when I wasn't there. She not only was beautiful, but well educated and was trying to break into the movie or theatre industry as a set designer. His ability to attract beautiful women to him was one of his true talents!

However, not being able to see and move easily deeply impacted the quality of his everyday life. He would tell me how he loved dreaming because in his dreams he could see perfectly.

At that time, the cancer metastasized and reached his bones, and he would need to be rushed to the hospital. I would either take him or meet him there. The imagery I was learning was being put to good use. I would pour light on my father and the doctors and nurses. Sometimes I would visualize him in nature, while we were in the emergency room. I was the only one allowed to stay in the emergency room as my father was visibly calmer when I was there, and so were the nurses and doctors. He would say to me, while the lights were very bright overhead, machines buzzing and some patient's wailing and moaning, "It's so peaceful in here." Oh, the power of imaginal light!

My father's death

My sister's visits became more of a necessity. Her adult daughter came to help as well. Both my sister and my cousin were getting upset that I was not spending more time with my father. The pull between my father and my two young girls was taking a toll. I felt torn in both directions and extremely guilty wherever I was: if with my daughters, I was not with my father; if with my father, I was not with my daughters. My husband's mother put her two cents in, and because she was one year younger than my father, her advice carried a lot of weight:

"Claudia, your two daughters need you now. I can see that they are upset at your absence. Your father is old enough to know better, he could allow other people to care for him."

It did not really stop the guilt or my trips in the middle of the night to the hospital, but it was helpful to hear an opinion from an elder family member. Eventually my father needed to be hospitalized and the doctors gently explained to me and to him that there was nothing they could do for him, the cancer had spread everywhere, and explained to him that he could go into hospice care where they would take care of any of his discomforts.

They showed him pictures of the hospice they were recommending, and, smiling, he said it looked like a good place. He asked how much it would cost. When they answered that it would be free, my father smiled broadly and said, "Now it looks perfect!"

And so, the man who would complain—if it were not one of his daughters or a beautiful woman taking care of him—gently gave permission to go to hospice!

My sister did not take to the news well. How could he be ready for hospice? She had just been there, in New York. He seemed fine! She was even more distraught when I called her after moving him to the hospice. I asked the nurses at the desk how long people are normally in hospice care. The nurse answered me, with some compassion; this question, I am sure, had been put to her before. "Sometimes, once they have decided to come here, it can take as little as three or four days."

My sister was in disbelief and angry. It couldn't be! She had just left! She couldn't come back so quickly.

"I know," I replied. "But it's what they said."

She calmed down after a day or two but could not come back right away. She came a week later. My father hung on, half unconscious. My sister went from the airport to the hospice. All who wanted to say good-bye came to see him that day or called on the phone; for some he would respond, for others not. He was incredibly sweet to my two daughters and managed to open his eyes.

My sister and I stayed with him after all the visitors had left, and around 10:00 p.m. I told her I would go home and come back early. She looked at me, and asked if I truly wanted to do that, and of course, at that moment it no longer seemed like a good idea.

Around 11 p.m., my father's breathing became labored and made a rattling sound. Frightened, I ran to the front desk where the male nurse calmed me, and told me that people choose carefully their day of death, that it is a date with meaning for them.

I went back to the room, I held one of my father's hands, my sister held the other. We told him of our love for him, so rhythmically and soothingly it was almost a lullaby. Even though he was not religious, a rabbi came and sang to him. I gently told him he would be going someplace, and not to be afraid. I could not tell if he could hear or understand us. We continued holding his hand as we tried to doze, putting our heads on our arms, resting them against the narrow hospital bed. My sister raised her head, and asked me if I knew the date. It was December 1, my mother's birthday! I knew that he would leave before midnight, and he did! My sister commented on how peaceful he looked when he passed.

After his passing my guilt was compounded! In very direct and not so direct ways, my sister and cousin were accusing me for being responsible for his death. The pain they felt devolved into blame. After an accusatory phone call, I told one of my father's doctors that my relatives felt I could have prevented the death. "Claudia, the cancer killed your father. There is nothing you did that could have stopped it or quickened it."

Still, a certain guilt wormed itself inward. My father had said to me, almost daily, "You will get cancer too!" Both he and my mother died of it. I would erase the suggestion. "Of course, I won't die of cancer," I thought. I know that what you believe has a big effect. I won't get cancer because I am aware, I am aware of emotional problems that can cause the cells to turn cancerous. "I am better than anyone who does get cancer," was my feeling. And that was part of the problem: the judgmental better-than-thou attitude.

Testing the imagery: my bout with cancer

"We cannot cure you if you don't get rid of guilt."
—Said the voice inside me

A year after his death, I was diagnosed with cancer of the uterine lining.

And thus, a year started of both incredible fear that I could die, and at some point, the awareness that I was being given gifts, gifts that I would not have been able to receive otherwise. I was being given a chance to work on whatever underlying emotional issues existed in me. And I would get the opportunity to test the imagery I was learning. However, the hopefulness emerged later, at first it was just fear.

What compounded the fear was that my cancer occurred at the same age my mother died of cancer, and at the same age that my grandmother died of a heart problem. I had a session with a woman who had experienced a spontaneous remission of her cancer and could 'see' beyond the here and now, and when she looked at me, she said she could see behind me a long line of women in my lineage that had died at 57. That terrified me.

What had I agreed to, what belief had I bought into? When I thought about my two adopted girls who had already been abandoned at birth, my body and mind railed. "No! I will not leave them. I don't know what I agreed to, but I can change my mind! Do you hear me? I will change my mind!"

Catherine had left for Europe for a busy schedule of workshops. Although she had given me excellent imagery exercises to deal with the cancer and the emotions and beliefs that needed to be addressed, dropped or changed, I felt a need to dip into other exercises, and to invent some. I was finally plunging into the work. I would see myself tearing up and burning contracts I had unconsciously made. "Whatever I decided," I yelled at the universe, "I am nullifying it, I no longer agree to it! No! I will not leave my daughters. No! It is not an option to die at age 57."

For 8 months I decided to not treat the cancer by conventional medical means. I was lucky in that my cancer cells were slow growing. I used imagery, diet, herbs, introspection and strong prayer. I cleaned house, as it were, both emotionally and physically. I told only four people I had cancer, my husband, Catherine, another student at the School of Images and my psychic friend, Patricia Masters. I knew that most people would object to my choice, and I did not want their reactions to fill me with fear. The surgeon was terrified for me but knew he could do nothing until I consented.

The cancer did not grow, but it did not diminish. One evening, as I was going to sleep and was doing my imagery exercises, I heard a voice from the inside:

"We cannot cure you if you don't get rid of guilt."

And so, the work I had been avoiding began in earnest. I talked to my parents, through imagery, through the ethers, as they had both passed, asking them to forgive me for what I felt I had done to them, how I had hurt them. They forgave me, but I realized as I did the work, that the person, who most needed to forgive me, was me. And so, I went through every instance of guilt, and would look at it honestly: did I mean the harm? Almost always I did not. And so, I forgave myself. As I did that work, I again heard, from the inside, that I must love myself as I really am, like God does. Once, using imagery in one of Catherine's classes, as the exercise guided, I took a peek at myself through God's eyes. I was stunned. He/She loved every part of me, even the parts I did not think were good or lovable. All of me was loved. I understood my 'bad' parts would help me; they were part of what would allow me to develop into all I was. I 'knew' it in feeling, not necessarily my mind. It was a truly felt sensation. I understood it in my bones, in my cells that all of me was loved.

At that point, I had a conversation with Patricia Masters, who seemed to call me at very crucial moments. We talked about surgery and chemo. I told her that if the cancer did not diminish I would go that route. She very sagely commented that it seemed that I believed that route would cure me, why didn't I just go in that direction now. I had a birth to attend to, a woman I had already committed to, and decided to wait until she gave birth. I called the surgeon and we scheduled an operation for June 1, two days before I turned 58!

The story was not over. I was terrified to lose my ovaries. Somewhere, somehow, I thought my physical ovaries were connected with my womanly compassionate feelings. What would happen to me if I didn't have them? The acupuncturist I was seeing explained to me that the body is very smart. When I lost my ovaries, all the hormones I would lose, would be compensated for by other organs. I didn't really believe him.

The surgeon insisted I see a psychologist to verify my decision. When I presented my dilemma to the psychologist, she brilliantly suggested I ask the ovaries. It had not occurred to me to do that! And so, I did. My ovaries were the most loving ovaries any woman could have! This is what they said, "Of course it is okay to take us out. It is for your greater good. Definitely. It is good to take us out." I do not know how to explain the love I felt from them. To this day, the love I felt from them moves me to tears.

I practiced the "The garden to prepare for procedures" exercise every day, to prepare for the operation. Friends and clients asked to be put into the garden as my protectors. Not only did I see all the doctors and their instruments in light, but I also decided to include another *DreamBirth* exercise, "Exchanging Parts with the Guardian Angel," and so I invited Archangel Michael to be at the operation. He would take all parts taken out of me, and return in their place, perfect parts made of light.

And every day, after the operation, I looked inside and my ovaries shone like stars. I never felt a loss. I felt a gain. I still have ovaries of light, 17 years later.

Three months after the operation, I was attending a CranioSacral workshop learning how to touch and sense the different organs. It was time to focus on the ovaries. The teacher would demonstrate on a student where the practitioners' hands should go, and what a healthy rhythm felt like. Each organ has its own particular, healthy rhythm. And if the rhythm is not optimal, he would show us how to encourage the better rhythm. Most of us know that the heart has an optimal rhythm, but so does every other organ. We all paired up, one of us was on the massage table, being the patient, while the other student became the practitioner. I was on the table, and as the 'practitioner' was following the instructions, I thought it best to let him know I did not have ovaries. He looked at me quizzically, as he was feeling the right rhythm. "Let me keep working, let me just see what I feel." He looked at me strangely. "I am feeling everything we are supposed to feel, quite strongly," he explained.

I told him about what I had done during the operation—that I had given myself ovaries of light. Part of the learning involves sensing at least two different people's organs, to experience the differences, and so we all rotated to work on one another. The initial practitioner came back to tell me, "Claudia, your ovaries of light have a much stronger rhythm than the other real ovaries!" My ovaries shone, especially bright, in gratitude.

But more importantly, having used the imagery to repair my body and transform my life, gave me, great expertise in the practice of imagery. What had been hearsay, those transformations that Catherine talked about, was now a living, breathing reality for me. There is not a day, not an hour, where I do not use imagery in one-way or another. The transformative and life-giving attributes of the imagery that I experienced transformed how I do the work, how I use this form of imagery. I know, beyond a shadow of a doubt, how profound and effective imagery is.

Believing

How do I know it's real, what I am seeing? Am I just making it up?

> *After that session, I no longer felt that emotional pull towards a third child. It was over. I had made my peace. I could now whole-heartedly jump into enjoying my present family, in its current composition, loving my two daughters and husband, not feeling there was something missing.*

Clients and students often ask me that. Claudia, how do I know I'm not just making this up? How do I know if it's real?

I know just how they feel. Sometimes the answer is simple: if possible, you verify what you 'saw.' If it is something in the future, you just need time. But what if it's something from the far past? Something you really do not know about, at least consciously?

For several years, when my daughters were still young, I had wanted to adopt a third child, insistently, passionately. I felt a third soul wanted to join the family. But my husband was afraid. A third child would break the budget, and if it was to be a boy, well, he didn't know what to do with boys. Please, Claudia, no. But the pull of the child was there. I looked at adoption applications. I talked to Patricia Masters, who was sure it would be a boy.

But I did not want to break my marriage. I did not want to adopt a third child without the full consent and cooperation of my husband. The dilemma pulled me in two directions, until finally I felt I had to decide, one way or the other.

Making a different agreement

I chose to keep my marriage intact, and so went to Catherine for help. In that session—after I explained that I felt the pull of a specific soul—she had me go 'in,' and explore who the person was. Perhaps it was possible to make a different agreement—this soul could come to me in a future lifetime. When I went 'in,' I saw a family, during pioneer times, in the United States. The house was wood, somewhat primitive and sparse. I was the daughter of the man who now wanted to be my child. We had loved each other, but life was very hard physically. We were never able to express the love. Nobody did in those times. I got married and left to go live with my husband. I never was able to see my father again or tell him about the love that I had for him.

And so, I talked to that soul of long- ago, about the love I had always felt. I told him that I was sorry I did not know how to express my love for him, and could we join again, with me being his mother, and he being my son, in another lifetime, not now? He understood. And so, a different agreement was made.

I felt crazed, as I was seeing those images. Was I making them up? Why the Wild West? What was this? And so, I now know how my clients and students feel. The verification happened when I stopped having that longing. Something must have genuinely happened. After that session, I no longer felt that emotional pull towards a third child. It was over. I had made my peace. I could now whole-heartedly jump into enjoying my present family, in its current composition, loving my two daughters and husband, not feeling there was something missing. I have not, since that session, wanted to adopt a third child.

I do not know if those images are accurate. I have no way to prove a past life or an ancestral memory. They are the pictures that came up, as opposed to any others that could have come up. But the verification lies in the result; I no longer feel that pull. That soul and I made a different agreement, for another lifetime. All is well. And as time passes the images ring truer and truer. I am sure I lived in those desolate, hard-working times. It feels accurate.

Intuition

Chapter 12
My universe within keeps expanding

Perhaps what most facilitates the communication between parent and baby is understanding and knowing that consciousness exists—before conception, during pregnancy and after miscarriage or abortion. There is no true end. And so, if all these souls have a reason, a soul purpose, well, then, each one of us does too.

As the stories illustrate, there is definitely more than meets the eye about conception, birth, miscarriage and abortion. It is apparent, when I learned how to listen, that we have a consciousness that does not end with physical death, and that we not only have a consciousness in the womb, we have one before we were conceived. This is not new knowledge.

Below is a story that came to me recently from several sources: a Facebook post,[23] a communication from an agent and book packager, and from the curriculum in the APPAH Pre-and-Perinatal training.

---

[23] This story has been passed around in Facebook, the same story, at different times. It was sent to me at the end of 2018, but it resides, as well, in Mindmovies.com, A Baby's Song (Special African Story).

The Himba tradition

The problem is that we have forgotten that each one of us has a song,
and that each one of us is unique and everlasting.
For when you recognize your own song, you have no desire or need
to do anything that would hurt another.

"Of all the African tribes still alive today, the Himba tribe is one of the few that counts the birth date of the children not from the day they are born nor conceived but the day the mother decides to have the child.

When a Himba woman decides to have a child, she goes off and sits under a tree, by herself, and she listens until she can hear the song of the child who wants to come. And after she's heard the song of this child, she comes back to the man who will be the child's father, and teaches him the song. When they make love to physically conceive the child, they sing the song of the child as a way of inviting the child.

When she becomes pregnant, the mother teaches that child's song to the midwives and the old women of the village, so that when the child is born, the old women and the people gather around him/her and sing the song to welcome the child. As the child grows up, the other villagers are taught the child's song. If the child falls, or gets hurt, someone picks him/her up and sings the song. Or maybe when the child does something wonderful, or goes through the rites of puberty then, as a way of honoring this person, the people of the village sing his or her song.

In the Himba tribe there is one other occasion when the "child song" is sung to the Himba tribesperson. If a Himba tribesman or tribeswoman commits a crime or something that is against the Himba social norms, the villagers call him or her into the center of the village and the community forms a circle around him/her. Then they sing their birth song.

The Himba views correction not as a punishment, but as love and remembrance of identity. For when you recognize your own song, you have no desire or need to do anything that would hurt another.

In marriage, the songs are sung, together. And finally, when the Himba tribesman/tribeswoman is lying in his/her bed, ready to die, all the villagers that know his or her song come and sing—for the last time that person's song."

The problem is that we have forgotten that each one of us has a song, and that each one of us is unique and everlasting. As women and their partners revealed themselves to me, the picture of loving souls creating helpful and healthful situations multiplied and became real. We seem to create situations that are miraculously designed to open our hearts and our minds.

Cancer was a perfect example of a situation that restored my heart and mind. Before the cancer diagnosis, I thought I was immune. After all, I thought, I knew all about the connection between the body and mind, and therefore (here is where my thinking became suspect) because of this knowledge, I reasoned, I am better than others. I did not believe that consciously, but the emotional connotations were clear in how I would respond to others who were sick. I would quickly think, feel that getting sick was not something I would do, and that in some way I was better. Many of us regard a quality we may have, for example, 'I am better educated,' 'I have better genes,' 'I come from a well-known family,' 'I am more creative,' and feel somehow that makes us better than those who do not have that quality.

When we feel we are better than others because of a quality, the Universe can step in with an experience that effectively 'corrects' our thinking. There is nothing wrong with acknowledging a quality. The problem is thinking we are better than others because of that quality. When I got cancer, the feeling that I was better than, didn't just dissolve, it exploded away. I was faced with my own humanity and with the raw fear that the cancer begat. It made me empathize with those who suffer and are plagued with intense fear. I knew what that felt like. And that indeed I was not better than anyone, but that I was equal to everyone, and that, in and of itself, is wonderful. It was understanding that we are all worthy beings, which nurtured and expanded compassion for others and myself. And this experience enabled me to let go of the guilt I chronically held inside and which had grown after my father's death. Had I not heard from inside that I needed to disengage from the guilt in order to be cured, I am not sure I would have tackled all the feelings of guilt and I-am-not-good enough that I harbored at that time.

The Universe gifted me with cancer so that I could in one fell swoop become more compassionate with myself and others, forgive myself for all my 'trespasses' and at the same time become more proficient in the imagery I use with others. Now I was using it for myself. Not only was I able to experience the benefits of the imagery directly but, with this new experience, I could give hope to many suffering from cancer. And that is what I call being efficient! Thank you, Universe.

Your mission is yours, not anybody else's

All these stories communicate and offer each one of us an expanded perspective: that we made a choice, or a series of choices and decisions, when we came into this life.

As I started to teach *DreamBirth* Imagery to other practitioners and birth professionals, and told the stories of these babies and what they had said, I would see in the student's faces, that their understanding of life was expanding.

Teaching *DreamBirth* to other professionals has made me realize this work is for anyone who has been in a womb, has a child in the womb or fervently wants a child in their womb. It is also for those who have suffered miscarriages or abortions. There is a way to communicate with these souls.

Perhaps what most facilitates the communication between parent and baby is understanding and knowing that consciousness exists—before conception, during pregnancy and after miscarriage or abortion. There is no true end. And so, if all these souls have a reason, a soul purpose, well, then, each one of us does too.

I, like so many, did not have the easiest of childhoods. That said there is no way I could have gained the optimism and hope that I now have, without the opportunity to transform those feelings of hopelessness and worthlessness into an awareness that the world is now mine and all is possible. I now truly believe that whatever I decide to do, I can do. But without having transformed my own life, and my own belief system, I could not be a good guide. The experience of transforming fear gave me authority in my work and in my teaching. The lack of attention, the emotional abandonment I experienced as a child has helped me help others traverse their victimhood. As I tell mothers who are afraid to repeat the way their own mothers treated them: realizing what did not feel good, enables us to find better ways to treat and parent our children.

I learned how to be with my daughters, enjoy them, pay attention to them, because my mother was not able to do that with me.

Adversity and challenges can polish us, bring out our best, and I have a suspicion that for many souls who are adventurous, having challenges is their true preference. They would rather have challenges than an easy life. Although I can imagine after many challenging lifetimes, a cushy, restful lifetime might be nice!

So, all choices work, no judgement here!

It is my hope that all who read this book will be touched with an expanded understanding and experience this expansion as strongly interwoven with love. As I do this work, my experience and perception of the 'universe' has changed. It is personal and loving. I do not need scientific proof. I feel the truth of it in my body. I see it in the stories of the women and men I have worked with and those who have presented themselves to me.

All these stories communicate and offer each one of us an expanded perspective: that we made a choice, or a series of choices and decisions, when we came into this life.

Some questions for the reader to ponder: If it is true that we choose our circumstances, why did you choose your parents? What did it give you? How did it form you, polish you? What did you learn to do, or perhaps to make sure not to do? There is no wrong answer, only right answers. Each one of us is unique; each one of us has his or her own song.

What did you come in to accomplish? Remember 'a mission' can be quite simple and profound: perhaps you came in to learn how to listen, or how to see what binds us instead of what separates us, or to heal family misunderstandings. Your mission is yours, not anybody else's. And when your soul's mission becomes your every day mission the wind is at your back, the universe supports you. Soul missions are always in the direction of more compassion, more love, and yes, more creativity and joy. As we are all connected, whether we believe that we are or not, our individual missions intertwine.

May each one of us hear our song, feel our inextricable connections, and play harmoniously together, in an ever expanding, never-ending symphony.

Tree of Life
Bruce des Peters

DreamBirth Exercises

"I credit the work with the growth of my intuitive and creative side, and in the fluidity of mind and imagination that the work engenders. I have learned that anyone can change their past, and I have truly experienced that."
—Mike, a future father

How to best 'do' the exercises **202**

Important Note re sex of child in the exercises **203**

Exercises to talk with your child in the womb **203**
    Going into the womb to visit your child 203

Exercises to talk to a soul miscarried or aborted **204**
    Entrusting your baby to the Holy Mother 204
    Cleaning out an abortion 205

Exercise to talk to your not as yet conceived baby! **206**
    To call forth a soul 206

Exercises in order of appearance **207**
    Secret garden 207
    My addition to the Garden Exercise 208
    Turning baby 208
    Cleaning your bedroom 209
    Freeing the inner child 210
    Rehearsing the birth—the flower. .210
    Cesarean 212
    Shining your ovaries and uterus 213
    Talking to a young child 214
    Holding the tree 215
    Clearing ancestral beliefs about conception 216
    Clearing your womb 217
    Ancestry support 218
    Secret garden for creating a safe space for the birth 218

Clearing ancestral trauma 220
The solar plexus 223
Meadow colors. 224
Clearing the field of the Donor Egg .224
Weaving your child's life tapestry and name 225
Repotting the plant 226
Clearing the office of the mind 227
Changing the Past 228
Reversing on Fear and Anxiety. 228
Tikkun Exercise 228
A New Past, New Present 229
A New Future 229
To call a soul that has passed 229
Reversing the past 230
Speaking to another's Higher Self 231
The castle 232
Looking at important males in your life 233
The chalice. 234
Taking your mother out of your body .235
The tide 235
The feather of truth 237
Return to a place of love 238
Stepping into someone else's shoes 239
Take three steps back 239
Blue vase 240
The garden—to prepare for procedures .241
Exchanging Parts with the Guardian Angel 243

How to best 'do' the exercises

As was mentioned in the Author's Note at the beginning of this book, these exercises are more effective if recited to you out loud, so you do not have to go in and out of your dreaming mind to read them to yourself. When someone else reads this to you, you can actively imagine and truly experience the images this practice elicits. I believe it is best of course, to work alongside a certified *DreamBirth* Practitioner, but the exercises will be beneficial any way you do them! (Certified practitioners are listed in the School of Images website, www.theschoolofimages.org.) If you are moved to read and 'do' the exercise on your own, Catherine's book, *DreamBirth: Transforming the Journey of Childbirth through Imagery*, is the very best guide for this use. Alternatively, you can, listen to the second volume of the audible version of *Messages from the Womb* where all the exercises have been recorded.

Remember that in doing this work what you 'see' or 'feel' in response to the exercises can involve your other senses, not only your visual sense. All that you feel in your body, with any of your senses—or even a sense of 'knowing' that comes from your soul is appropriate. So do not worry if you cannot 'see.' This often develops over time. When I began as a body worker I would mainly sense things kinesthetically. I 'knew' what part of the client's body needed my attention. Without any effort on my part as I started to work with this type of imagery, I could both kinesthetically sense where I needed to go, and clearly 'see' where I needed to go. Many doula clients who could not 'see' when we worked together during their first pregnancy were absolute whizzes when they worked with me again during their second pregnancy. Their 'seeing' had dramatically developed, and their images were vibrant and clear. All your senses 'see,' and how you respond to the exercises is your way, and appropriate, and may change with time!

Important Note re sex of child in the exercises

In *DreamBirth*, Catherine alternated, in the exercises, the sex of the child, Chapter by Chapter. In one Chapter the baby is a she, in the next the baby is a he. The choice of sex can be more fluid, and of course very specific to you, so when you use these exercises, please use the pronoun that best fits: whether it is he, his, she, hers or they, or any combination that most pleases you.

Exercises to talk with your child in the womb

Going into the womb to visit your child
(Introduced in Chapter 4 with Julia)

Breathe out slowly three times, counting from 3 to 1, seeing the numbers in your mind's eye. See the number 1 as tall, clear and bright.

Turn your eyes inward to travel down to your womb. Your eyes shine like two beams illuminating your way down inside your body to the amniotic sac. When you are there, bring your eyes close to the transparent membrane of the sac and look at your baby floating freely in its clear blue amniotic waters.

Breathe out. Talk to your baby (later on, when your baby has reached the stage of development when her eyes are open, make eye contact with her while talking). Tell your baby all you want to tell her, using words or images. Tell her how much you love her, how much you are looking forward to her arrival.

Breathe out. Tell her of any particular stresses or shocks you may be experiencing. Tell her not to worry, that all is well, that she's safe inside the amniotic sac, tucked under your heart.

Breathe out. Remind your baby of the particular phase of development she's in right now (according to the chart) and visualize the perfect development of that part of her body. (Remember that the phase changes each week, so keep in touch with the weekly changes and visualize them happening perfectly.)

Breathe out. Tell your baby you have to go now but that you'll be back to visit again at lunch and diner times. Tell her that, even though you may be busy with other things, she's safely in your body and being taken care of.

Breathe out. Bring your eyes back up into your sockets.

Breathe out. Open your eyes, registering the room around you while also seeing with open eyes your baby tucked comfortably under your heart.

DreamBirth: Transforming the Journey of Childbirth through Imagery by Catherine Shainberg. Published by Sounds True, ©2014. All rights reserved. Exercise 28, page 66. http://www.SoundsTrue.com Reprinted with permission of publisher.

And of course, if you start this exercise after much of their development has occurred, remember that cells are responsive and fluid, they will respond appropriately if you admire their perfect development. Do not worry that you did not urge the cells from the very beginning of the baby's development. The baby's cells will be very happy to get the message of how perfect they are, at any point in their development and will respond to the message, and become perfect and whole. Remember that cells renew themselves all the time.

Exercises to talk to a soul miscarried or aborted

Entrusting your baby to the Holy Mother
(Introduced in Chapter 4 with Julia)

Close your eyes. Breathe out slowly three times, counting from 3 to 1, seeing the numbers in your mind's eye. See the number 1 as tall, clear, and bright.

See the soul that has left your body and ask it to show you in images or tell you in words what made it go away and what, if any, corrections need to be done for the soul to be able to return.

Breathe out. If the soul doesn't intend to return, ask it if it has accomplished what it needed to do in this world in its very brief incarnation.

Breathe out. If the soul doesn't intend to return, tell it your grief and sorrow at its passing and your wishes for its well-being.

Breathe out. Ask if another soul is intending to come. Thank it for the information.

Breathe out. Now take the hand of the child that left and together jump into a white cloud in the sky. Ask the cloud to take you to the Holy Mother.

Breathe out. See the Holy Mother approaching, surrounded by many angelic beings. Give her your precious child to safeguard.

Breathe out. Say your last good-byes. Watch as your child is taken up by the Holy Mother and the angels to play in the water pools in the sky with the many other babies.

Breathe out. Hear your child laughing with the other children. Return down to earth knowing she is well taken care of.

Breathe out and open your eyes.

©2005 Dr. Catherine Shainberg

Cleaning out an abortion

(Introduced in Chapter 5 with Isabel)

Close your eyes. Breathe out slowly three times, counting from 3 to 1, seeing the numbers in your mind's eye. See the number 1 as tall, clear, and bright.

Call on the soul of your lost child. You can see it appearing as a pair of little red shoes. Ask your child to forgive you, explaining to her the reasons for your actions, (e.g., you couldn't support the child, you weren't married, you were selfish, you were too young, or your parents would be angry). Give all the reasons.

Breathe out. Hear what the child says. If the child won't forgive you, ask what she needs you to do or promise her in order for her to forgive.

Breathe out. Once you have made an agreement (life-affirming for you and acceptable to her), thank the child for her forgiveness and promise her that from now on, you will respect life.

Breathe out. Ask the child if she intends to come back to you. Tell the child now is a time when you can receive her safely. Hear what she says.

Breathe out. Say goodbye to your child and see the little red shoes moving away and disappearing.

Breathe out. Open your eyes, feeling absolved and open to the future.

Exercise to talk to your not as yet conceived baby!

To call forth a soul

(Introduced in My Addition to the Garden Exercise section)

Close your eyes. Breathe out slowly three times, counting from 3 to 1, seeing the numbers in your mind's eye. See the number 1 as tall, clear, and bright.

Imagine that you are standing in a meadow looking up at the sky on a clear day. See a white cloud floating gently out from the left side of the blue sky and see the soul of your child appearing on this cloud.

Breathe out. When your child appears, ask him what you need to do to prepare for his arrival. What changes must you make in your physical, emotional and mental bodies for your child to be able to incarnate? Pay great attention to the answer.

Breathe out. When you have heard and seen, promise your child to promptly do what is necessary to secure his arrival. Thank him for being patient.

Breathe out. Open your eyes.

Exercises in order of appearance

Secret garden
(Introduced in Chapter 2: Babies add to the Garden)

Close your eyes. Breathe out slowly three times, counting from 3 to 1, seeing the numbers in your mind's eye. See the number 1 as tall, clear, and bright.

Imagine that you are standing in front of a circular walled garden. Walk around the walls until you find the gate. Find the key to the gate and unlock the gate.

Breathe out. Walk into the garden. What does it look like? Are there flowers? What colors? How do they smell?

Breathe out. If the garden needs tending, do so until the garden looks just as you want it to look.

Breathe out. Walk deeper into the garden, toward the center. Find a beautiful strong tree that offers shade and sit in its shade on a patch of thick emerald- green grass.

Breathe out. Listen for water nearby. Hear the sounds of nature. Feel yourself breathing with nature, in rhythm with its cycles.

Breathe out. Feel and see your baby responding to your breathing as he also becomes attuned to the rhythms of nature.

Breathe out. Rest and relax, enjoying nature and your baby until you feel rejuvenated.

Breathe out. Get up and walk back out of your garden, your baby safely tucked under your heart. Notice whether anything looks different as you go.

Breathe out. Close the gate behind you and lock it, taking the key or hiding it in some safe place where you can find it whenever you need it.

Breathe out. Open your eyes, asking that the feeling of rest and peacefulness continue for both of you throughout your day.

My addition to the Garden Exercise

I often do the "Secret garden" with clients after doing "Going into the womb to visit your child." Then, when in the Garden, after the woman has rejuvenated (as the exercise prescribes or suggests), I ask her to go in to visit the baby in the womb again, and ask the baby if there is anything he or she would like in the garden. What the babies say is quite specific, and more than anything secures the bond between the mother and the child. It is often a 'jolt' to everyone in the room, as the baby has very specific likes and dislikes!

After a child has been seen in "To call forth a child," we often invite the soul— the child yet to be—into the Garden, and again ask the child if there is anything they would like in the garden.

Turning baby
(Introduced in Chapter 3 with Lindsay)

Close your eyes. Breathe out slowly three times, counting from 3 to 1, seeing the numbers in your mind's eye. See the number 1 as tall, clear, and bright.

See yourself in a meadow. It's a bright sunny day.

Breathe out. Stretch your arms out toward the sun, feel them elongating until your hands are very close to the sun. See your hands becoming very warm and turning into light.

Breathe out. Now feel your arms returning to their natural length.

Breathe out. Bring your hands inside your body to the amniotic sac. Gently and carefully take hold of the sac and move it until your baby is in the ideal position for birth—head down and facing toward your back, cord floating up loosely.

Breathe out. Take your hands out of your body and place them on your belly. Send warmth and reassurance to your baby that this is the correct and ideal position for birth.

Breathe out. With open eyes, see your baby in the ideal position for birth.

DreamBirth: Transforming the Journey of Childbirth through Imagery by Catherine Shainberg. Published by Sounds True, ©2014. All rights reserved. Exercise 73, page 147. http://www. SoundsTrue.com   Reprinted with permission of publisher.

Cleaning your bedroom
(Introduced in Chapter 4 with Jennifer)

Close your eyes. Breathe out slowly three times, counting from 3 to 1, seeing the numbers in your mind's eye. See the number 1 as tall, clear, and bright.

Imagine you are gathering your supplies—broom, sponge, duster, pail of soapy waters—to clean your bedroom.

Breathe out. Begin to clean, sensing every movement of your body as you scrub the ceiling, the walls, from top to bottom, the windows inside and out.

Breathe out. Open closets and chest of drawers, putting everything you no longer need or find useful into a large black garbage bag. Dust and clean the closets and drawers.

Breathe out. Take the rugs to the window and beat the dust out of them.

Breathe out. Move the furniture. Turn the mattress over. Wash the floor.

Breathe out. When you have finished cleaning your room, rearrange the furniture.

Breathe out. Now place what you mean to keep in closets and drawers. Make your bed with clean, new sheets.

Breathe out. Take all your supplies and wash or clean them before putting them away.

Breathe out. Carry the black garbage bag out to a garbage truck, throw it into the truck, and watch as it is crushed. Then watch the truck drive away.

Breathe out. When you have completely cleared and rearranged your bedroom to your satisfaction, find and bring into your room a special object or flower arrangement that gives you pleasure and enhances the room.

Breathe out. Open your eyes, seeing your clean new bedroom with open eyes.

DreamBirth: Transforming the Journey of Childbirth through Imagery by Catherine Shainberg. Published by Sounds True, ©2014. All rights reserved. Exercise 7, page 22. http://www. SoundsTrue.com Reprinted with permission of publisher.

Freeing the inner child

(Introduced in Chapter 4 with Jennifer)

(Not always mentioned by name, "Freeing the Inner child," is a very useful exercise when an unhappy incident from childhood comes up. Even if the unhappiness is coming from a present event, a little questioning about when they first had the feeling, often elicits memories from the past.)

Close your eyes. Breathe out slowly three times, counting from 3 to 1, seeing the numbers in your mind's eye. See the number 1 as tall, clear, and bright.

Tell your child that you are going to do an exercise now, that whatever emotions you feel should not concern her, that all is well and she is safe in her amniotic sac, tucked comfortably under your heart.

See the child in you. Where is she? What is she doing? Take care of whatever necessity appears. For instance, if the child is in a corner crying, do what is necessary to console her.

Breathe out. Take her out into a meadow to run and play. Play with her. Tell her she is now free to have fun, and that you will play with her.

Breathe out and open your eyes.

DreamBirth: Transforming the Journey of Childbirth through Imagery by Catherine Shainberg. Published by Sounds True, ©2014. All rights reserved. Exercise 57, page 117. http://www. SoundsTrue.com Reprinted with permission of publisher.

Rehearsing the birth—the flower

(Introduced in Chapter 4 with Jennifer)

Close your eyes. Breathe out slowly three times, counting from 3 to 1, seeing the numbers in your mind's eye. See the number 1 as tall, clear, and bright.

Turn your eyes inward into your body. Your eyes are very bright, illuminating the way. Travel down to the amniotic sac.

Breathe out. When you come to it, look in to see your baby floating freely and comfortably in the clear blue amniotic waters.

Breathe out. Make eye contact with your baby, smile, and talk to her, telling her everything you want to say today.

Breathe out. Tell your baby that you and she are going to rehearse her birth. You are going to show her exactly what will happen when she is ready to be born. Tell your baby how excited you are at the thought of soon seeing her face and holding her in your arms. You are going to lead your baby through a visualization of her perfect birth.

Breathe out. Visualize your baby turning to be head down, face toward your sacrum, in the perfect birthing position. See that the cord is floating upward from the belly button, free and unencumbered, and will remain so throughout the birth.

Breathe out. See that your baby's head is resting at the stem of an upside-down flower whose bud is beginning to open up slowly, petal by petal, until the flower is completely and widely open.

Breathe out. Now visualize your baby sliding down the stem of the flower in a rush of waters and lubricating oils, cord floating up freely.

Breathe out. See your baby come out through the wide opening of the flower into a magnificent garden and into your partner's arms.

Breathe out. See your partner placing your baby on your chest. Feel the exhilaration and joy as you hold her in your arms and look at her face for the first time. Hear all of nature rejoicing in the arrival of your newborn.

Breathe out and open your eyes.

Cesarean

(Introduced in Chapter 4 with Jennifer)

(For your safety as well as the baby's)

Close your eyes. Breathe out slowly three times, counting from 3 to 1, seeing the numbers in your mind's eye. See the number 1 as tall, clear, and bright.

You are walking around the base of a circular wall. Above the wall, you see the tops of trees. Walk until you find the gate. The key is in the lock: open the gate and walk into the garden.

Breathe out. What does your garden look like? If you are not satisfied with the way it looks, repair your garden.

Breathe out. Walk deeper into the garden and find a patch of very thick, soft, emerald-green grass next to a tree and a running brook.

Breathe out. Lie on the grass in the shade of the tree and listen to the sounds of the brook and the birds. Feel how your body rhythms become attuned to the rhythms of nature.

Breathe out. Now invite those you trust to come into the garden, one by one, and sit in a semicircle around your head. Feel their love and attentiveness.

Breathe out. When all of your witnesses have come in and sat down around you, and when you feel comfortable and at ease, show your body in a precise visualization exactly what is going to happen during the C-section. Ask your body's permission to allow this procedure and remind your body that the C-section is being recommended by your doctor.

Breathe out. If your body refuses permission, ask your body what it needs to make this possible. Respond to the necessity of your body in images.

Once your body has given permission, invite your doctor, assistants, and nurses to come into the garden with their medications and tools. When they stand before you, see how the sunlight pours down onto their heads and into their arms and hands so that everything they touch—medication, tools, your body—turns to light.

Breathe out. See that all is done perfectly. Your baby comes out healthy and whole and is placed on your chest. Smile at your baby and feel that all is well.

Breathe out. When the cord is cut, the placenta lifted away, and your cut stitched up, and the doctor has finished all that must be done, see the doctor, assistants and nurses leaving.

Breathe out. Feel all of your loved ones still around you, guarding and protecting you; feel their presence and their joy. When you are ready, let them go one by one out of the garden. The gate closes on the last one, and you are alone with your baby and your partner.

Breathe out. Feel the rhythms of nature, feel your body and your baby breathing with the rhythms of nature.

Breathe out. When you are ready, get up with your baby in your arms and together with your partner, slowly walk out of your garden, close the gate, and take the key or put it in a place where you will always be able to find it.

Breathe out. Walk into your future with your baby in your arms, your partner by your side.

DreamBirth: Transforming the Journey of Childbirth through Imagery by Catherine Shainberg. Published by Sounds True, ©2014. All rights reserved. Exercise 68, page 137. http://www. SoundsTrue.com   Reprinted with permission of publisher.

Shining your ovaries and uterus
(Introduced in Chapter 4 with Julia)

Close your eyes. Breathe out slowly three times, counting from 3 to 1, seeing the numbers in your mind's eye. See the number 1 as tall, clear, and bright.

Imagine that you are standing in a meadow on a clear, sunny day. Look up at the sun. Stretch your arms toward the sun, feel them getting longer and longer. Feel your hands getting warm, your fingers turning into light. See a little hand appearing at the tip of each finger. Now you have fifty little fingers of light.

Breathe out. Bring your fifty little fingers down into your body to illuminate your ovaries.

Breathe out. Start massaging one of your ovaries with your fifty little fingers of light until your ovary becomes as bright and shining as a star.

Breathe out. Massage the other ovary until it, too, is as bright and shining as a star.

Breathe out. Lift your hands up to the sun again. Feel the little hands disappearing back into your fingers. Gather a bouquet of sun rays. Bring it down to you as your arms return to their normal length.

Breathe out. Roll the sun rays into a perfect ball of sunlight. Put it into your uterus. See it rolling around the inside of your uterus, clearing whatever needs to be cleared and coating it with golden oil.

Breathe out. Return the ball of sunlight to the sun.

Breathe out. Open your eyes, seeing your two starry ovaries and the sun of your uterus with open eyes.

DreamBirth: Transforming the Journey of Childbirth through Imagery by Catherine Shainberg. Published by Sounds True, ©2014. All rights reserved. Exercise 22, page 48. http://www. SoundsTrue.com   Reprinted with permission of publisher.

Talking to a young child
(Introduced in Chapter 4 with Julia)
(When child seems upset, perhaps clingy and insecure about birth or upcoming of younger sibling.)

Close your eyes. Breathe out slowly three times, counting from 3 to 1, seeing the numbers in your mind's eye. See the number 1 as tall, clear, and bright.

Call upon the soul of your eldest child. See your child appear.

Breathe out. Ask your child if there is anything that is bothering him or her. Is there anything your child would like you to know or to tell you? (You may see it in images, not necessarily words.)

Breathe out. Respond if necessary, and continue the conversation until it feels resolved.

Breathe out. Tell your child that you want to show him (or her) the bridge of love that exists between the two of you, that it's a bridge that can't be broken or made smaller no matter how many brothers of sisters there are.

Breathe out. Tell your child that a mother's love gets even bigger when more siblings come into the picture.

Breathe out. Turn your eyes into your heart and see the color of your feeling for your child. When you see the color of your feeling for your child send the color as a bridge of light from your heart to your child's heart. Pour all the love you have for your child onto this bridge.

Breathe out. Ask your child if he can feel the love. If not, pour more love. (I've never had a child say no.)

Tell your child you are going to play a game, to see how far the bridge can go.

Breathe out. And ask your child to jump up to a nearby cloud.

Breathe out. Send all the love you have for him again, and ask your child if he can feel your love. (It has always been a yes).

Breathe out. Now ask your child to jump onto a star. Send your love again, and ask your child if he can feel it.

Breathe out. Ask the child to come back down, and now you, the mother, jump onto a nearby cloud. Again, send your love. Ask the child if he can feel your love. (Depending on what the problem is, I improvise: can the child feel the mother's love when the mother is at work, can the child feel the mother's love when the mother is holding the other sibling, and so on.)

Breathe out and open your eyes. (Claudia Raiken)

© 2019 Claudia Raiken

Holding the tree
(Introduced in Chapter 4 with Caterina)

Close your eyes. Breathe out slowly three times, counting from 3 to 1, seeing the numbers in your mind's eye. See the number 1 as tall, clear, and bright.

Imagine that you have walked deep into the woods on a sunny, warm and pleasant day. Feel the dappling sun shine through the canopies of the trees.

Hear the sounds of nature. Hear your footsteps, as you walk deeper into the woods. Come to a little opening where there are a number of trees. Looking around, choose the tree that attracts you the most. Look at it carefully so that you can describe it to yourself.

Breathe out. Go up to the tree. Put your arms around the trunk of the tree and lay your left cheek against the bark. Listen to the sound of the tree.

Breathe out. Feel all the sensations of the bark on your skin, the smell of the tree. Holding the tree with your arms and hands, listen deeper and hear what the tree is telling you.

Breathe out. When you have heard what it has to say, step away from the tree. Walk backwards until you can see the whole tree again. Take a look at it now. What does it look like, what, if anything has changed?

Breathe out. What do you look like, and how do you feel now?

Breathe out. Keep the message of the tree preciously with you as you retrace your steps through the woods. Is there anything different in your journey back through the woods? Note the differences.

Breathe out and, open your eyes

©2005 Dr. Catherine Shainberg

Clearing ancestral beliefs about conception
(Introduced in Chapter 5 with Isabel)

Close your eyes. Breathe out slowly three times, counting from 3 to 1, seeing the numbers in your mind's eye. See the number 1 as tall, clear, and bright.

Imagine that you are in the house of your ancestors. Climb up to the attic, look around, and find the old chest that you have been told contains your family's ancestral beliefs about conception and childbirth.

Breathe out. Open the chest. What do you find?

Breathe out. Keep what you like and discard the rest. Make a pile of what you are discarding and take it out to the garden to burn. Then bury the ashes.

Breathe out. Walk away with what you have kept.

Breathe out. Open your eyes.

DreamBirth: Transforming the Journey of Childbirth through Imagery by Catherine Shainberg. Published by Sounds True, ©2014. All rights reserved. Exercise 12, page 30. http://www. SoundsTrue.com Reprinted with permission of publisher.

Clearing your womb
(Introduced in Chapter 5 with Paz)

Close your eyes. Breathe out slowly three times, counting from 3 to 1, seeing the numbers in your mind's eye. See the number 1 as tall, clear, and bright.

Turning your eyes inward, let your gaze travel down into your womb. See all the cords that still attach you to former partners.

Breathe out. Identifying each cord with a former partner, thank the man for what he has taught you, then firmly cut the cord that still attaches you to him, knowing that you are returning his energy to him and, in the process, restoring your own completeness.

Breathe out. Continue doing this for each cord until all are cut.

Breathe out. Pour fresh spring water in your womb. See your womb as clean and bright.

Breathe out. Feel refreshed and restored to wholeness, ready to receive your partner of choice, the one your heart has singled out to be the father of your child.

Breathe out. Open your eyes.

DreamBirth: Transforming the Journey of Childbirth through Imagery by Catherine Shainberg. Published by Sounds True, ©2014. All rights reserved. Exercise 6, page 21. http://www. SoundsTrue.com Reprinted with permission of publisher.

Ancestry support

(Introduced in Chapter 5 with Paz)

Close your eyes. Breathe out slowly three times, counting from 3 to 1, seeing the numbers in your mind's eye. See the number 1 as tall, clear, and bright.

See the women around you who are positive and supportive.

See their faces. How many are there?

Breathe out. Behind your women friends, see your female ancestors all the way back to Eve.

Breathe out. Have them surround you and hold you from behind.

Sense and know that the Divine Mother is behind all of them, supporting them in supporting you. Sink back into their arms and let yourself be held.

Breathe out. Open your eyes, feeling the support with open eyes.

DreamBirth: Transforming the Journey of Childbirth through Imagery by Catherine Shainberg. Published by Sounds True, ©2014. All rights reserved. Exercise 55, page 112. http://www.SoundsTrue.com   Reprinted with permission of publisher.

Secret garden for creating a safe space for the birth

(Introduced in Chapter 6 with Marisa)
(This exercise is based on, "The Garden to Prepare for Procedures," exercise 156, page 287, in *DreamBirth*, and is included later on in this Glossary. I changed the exercise to fit a natural birth. It is very important to ask permission of the body and the baby for any interventions that may need to happen for the health of the baby or the birthing woman.)

Close your eyes. Breathe out slowly three times, counting from 3 to 1, seeing the numbers in your mind's eye. See the number 1 as tall, clear, and bright.

You are walking around what looks like a circular wall. Above the wall, you see the tops of trees. Walk until you find the gate. The key is in the lock. Open the gate and walk into the garden.

Breathe out. What does your garden look like? If the garden needs some tending, do so until the garden looks just as you want it to look.

Breathe out. Walk deeper into the garden and find a patch of thick, soft, emerald-green grass next to a tree and a running brook.

Breathe out. Lie on the grass in the shade of the tree and listen to the sounds of the brook and the birds, feeling how your body rhythms become attuned to the rhythms of nature.

Breathe out. Invite into the garden, one by one, the people in your life you trust and want to have present to serve as your protectors and energy-keepers, including loved ones who have passed. Feel their love and support. Sense it in every cell of your body.

Breathe out. Now invite the doctor (or midwife), any assistants, and nurses who will be there, into the garden. As they stand before you, see how golden light from the sun pours down on their heads and travels down to their hands, which become filled with light. See that everything they touch—your body, the bed, any instruments, medications (if any will be needed)—turns to light. See that they are well grounded in light, and all they do is done perfectly, guided by the light.

Breathe out. Turn your eyes inward to your body and ask the cells of your body if they are willing to cooperate with what needs to happen for an easy vaginal birth.

Thank your cells for their co-operation.

Breathe out. And now ask the cells of your body if they will co-operate with any intervention (including a cesarean birth) that may be needed for the well-being of you and the baby. Thank them for their co-operation.

Breathe out. Now see the baby in the perfect position. Visualize your baby turning to be head down, face towards your sacrum, chin gently tucked, her arms crossed at the chest, in the perfect birthing position. See that the cord is floating upward from her belly button, free and unencumbered and will remain so throughout the birth.

Breathe out. See that your baby's head is resting at the opening to the stem of an upside-down flower whose bud is beginning to open up slowly, petal by petal, till the flower is completely and widely open.

Breathe out. Now visualize your baby sliding down the stem of the flower in a rush of waters and lubricating oils, cord floating up freely.

Breathe out. See your baby come out through the wide opening of the flower into the garden and into her father's (modify when necessary) arms. Breathe out. See him placing your baby on your chest. Feel the exhilaration and joy as you hold your baby in your arms.

Breathe out. Feel the rejoicing of all who love you, and the rejoicing of the nature around you, welcoming your baby into this world. See your baby's face, hands, fingernails. See how she (he) looks into your eyes and follows her (his) father's voice. See, feel the connection you already have with your baby. See the connection the baby already has with each one of you.

And now, thanking the doctor (or midwife), nurses and assistants, see them leave the garden. Breathe out. Feel the presence and love of those who have been watching over you and your new child. When you are ready, have them leave the garden one by one, thanking them, and listening to any message they may have for you.

Breathe out. Now you are alone in your garden (or with your partner and child). Listen to the sounds of nature, the water, the birds, the insects, the breeze. Watch the play of light and shadow in the leaves of your tree. Feel yourself at peace and in rhythm with nature.

Breathe out. When you are ready, get up, feel the thick elastic, emerald- green grass under your bare feet. Slowly, enjoying the sights and scents of your garden, walk out, close the gate, and take the key or put it in a place you will always be able to find it.

Breathe out. Feeling whole and healthy, walk away.

Breathe out and open your eyes.

DreamBirth: Transforming the Journey of Childbirth through Imagery by Catherine Shainberg. Published by Sounds True, ©2014. All rights reserved. Exercise 156, page 287. http://www. SoundsTrue.com   Reprinted with permission of publisher.
(with a few changes by Claudia Raiken)

Clearing ancestral trauma
(Introduced in Chapter 7 with Patricia)
(This is best done with a certified practitioner of *DreamBirth*.)

Close your eyes. Breathe out slowly three times, counting from 3 to 1. See the 1 tall, clear, and bright.

Recognize a recurring pattern in your life. Observe whether this is also a familial pattern.

Breathe out. Return back through your life, noting the pattern as it occurs. Do this fast. Do not linger.

Breathe out. Go to the very first time in your life that you observe this pattern. How old are you? Where are you? Who else is there? What is the event?

Breathe out. Cut the cord between you and the other person(s).

Breathe out. Return into your mother's womb. Return backward through the gestational development, watching to see whether you experience the same emotions that are consistent with this pattern. Note the gestational ages when you feel it most strongly.

Breathe out. Go back to the time of conception. What feelings do you experience?

Breathe out. Go back to before incarnation. Look down at your two parents and ask what attracted you to them.

Breathe out. Ask, what is your mission in life? Make sure to clearly recognize your mission before moving on.

Breathe out. Turn 180 degrees. Looking at the familial dreamfields of your father and of your mother; ask which one needs to be addressed to clear this recurring pattern you are working on. See the DreamField that needs to be addressed lighting up.

Breathe out. Ask to be taken directly to the very first event that triggered this pattern, and its repetition down the family line. This event could have happened many generations ago. (Trust your dreaming, and the images you are being shown.) Describe exactly what is happening, who it is happening to. Describe everything you are shown about the event.

Breathe out three times counting from three to one. Roll back this person's life to show you what was happening before this traumatic event occurred.

Breathe out. Roll this person's life forward. How has the event impacted this person's life? What has this person's life been like since the damaging event?

Breathe out. Come to the person's time of death. What are this person's feelings and thoughts at the time of passing?

Breathe out three times counting from three to one. You, today, go and stand next to your ancestor as they experience the traumatic event. Tell your ancestor you are going to cut the cord that has held their soul, and all the souls of the family lineage, in bondage to this memory.

Breathe out. Call on the great force of transformation that you can visualize as the archangel Michael. See the blue sky opening, Michael descending, dressed in his saphire *blue robe, holding the* saphire *blue sword of fire.*

Breathe out. Ask his permission to borrow the sword.

Breathe out. Using Michael's sword cut the cord connecting this ancestor to the traumatic event. See what happens to the perpetrator(s) or to the scene.

Breathe out. If the perpetrator(s) is/are still there, continue cutting invisible cords until the perpetrator(s) has/have gone or dissolved.

Breathe out. Tell your ancestor that their soul is now free and can go where souls live. Watch as the soul leaves.

Breathe out three times counting from three to one. There is a bucket of water at your feet. Plunge the tip of the sword into the water. See the saphire *blue fire charging the water. Now you have firewater.*

Breathe out. Return the sword to Michael, thanking him. Ask for his blessing.

Breathe out. Feel his hand on your head. See and feel the saphire blue fire passing through every cell in your body, clearing and cleansing it of this old pattern. The fire will stop running through your body when it is done.

Breathe out. See your cells returning to their natural healthy alignment.

Breathe out. Look into the eyes of the Archangel and hear his blessing.

Breathe out. Watch as he returns into his heavenly abode.

Breathe out three times counting from three to one. See the line of your ancestors all the way down to your children and their children, cousins, nephews and nieces, and their children.

Breathe out. Take the firewater and throw it down the line. Watch what happens to the lineage.

Breathe out. There is one drop left in the bucket. Pick it up on the tip of your index finger, and place it on your body where the body wants it.

Breathe out. Open your eyes, knowing the repair is done and the pattern cleared out for you, for all your ancestry and for your living and future family members.

The Kabbalah of Light by Catherine Shainberg. Published by Inner Traditions International and Bear & Company, ©2022. All rights reserved. Exercise 65, pages 176–178. http://www.Innertraditions.com   Reprinted with permission of publisher.

The solar plexus

(Introduced in Chapter 7 with Patricia)

Close your eyes. Breathe out slowly three times, counting from 3 to 1. See the 1 tall, clear, and bright.

Imagine that you're standing in your meadow. Look up at the blue sky, and see where the sun is. If the sun is to your left, watch as the sun travels across the sky until it reaches noontime and the sun is right above you.

Breathe out. Elongate your arms toward the sun, feel your hands getting warm, turning to light.

Breathe out. Catch the sun in your two hands, and bring it down. Put it in your solar plexus. See it igniting the sun in your body, then quickly put the sun back in the sky.

Breathe out. See the sun ignited in your solar plexus , radiating out in all directions. See it as a great wheel of light. See how others are attracted to your light and warmth and start walking toward you from all directions.

Breathe out. Open your eyes.

The Kabbalah of Light by Catherine Shainberg. Published by Inner Traditions International and Bear & Company, ©2022. All rights reserved. Exercise 45, page 143. http://www.Innertraditions.com   Reprinted with permission of publisher.

Meadow colors

(Introduced in Chapter 7 with Patricia)

Close your eyes. Breathe out slowly three times, counting from 3 to 1, seeing the numbers in your mind's eye. See the number 1 as tall, clear, and bright.

See that you are in a large, very lush green meadow. On the other side of the meadow, see your partner. Feel excited and happy to see him.

Breathe out. As you walk toward each other see what color he emanates, what color you emanate.

Breathe out. See the colors getting more and more vibrant and warmer. See him becoming a brighter and brighter red and see yourself becoming more and more brightly orange.

Breathe out. When you meet and the two colors come together, see what is created.

Breathe out. Open your eyes, seeing what is created with open eyes.

DreamBirth: Transforming the Journey of Childbirth through Imagery by Catherine Shainberg. Published by Sounds True, ©2014. All rights reserved. Exercise 24, page 51. http://www. SoundsTrue.com   Reprinted with permission of publisher.

Clearing the field of the Donor Egg

(Introduced in Chapter 7 with Patricia)

(For a mother planning In Vitro Fertilization)

Close your eyes. Breathe out slowly three times, counting from 3 to 1, seeing the numbers in your mind's eye. See the number 1 as tall, clear, and bright.

Imagine that you connect with the woman donating her egg.

Connect to her higher soul, asking the donor's permission to clear her ancestral field so that the donated egg will be cleansed of all negative imprints.

Breathe out. See that the donor's ancestral field is a veil that stretches across the whole of your vision. Look at the veil and see whether it is clean or not. If it is not clean, take a pail of clear clean water and throw the water on the veil again and again until it is clean.

If there is some necessity to clear your field, do it now.

Breathe out. Ask if the donor's higher soul gives permission to donate her egg.

If she says yes, breathe out slowly and see a spark of light that is the egg jumping out of the donor's field and entering into your field.

Breathe out. See how the donor's egg and your field interweave and become one. See that the egg is finely vibrating at a speed and in a way that fits this new field. See how they come to a rhythmic interaction that works for both.

Breathe out, and ask your womb if it is ready to receive this new egg now that the ancestral field has been cleansed.

If your body says yes, breathe out slowly and see the dome of the sky descending over you. See the spark that is the egg jumping into your womb where it shines brightly. As soon as you have seen and felt the spark in your womb, the dome of the sky returns up into the heavens.

Breathe out and see yourself sitting under a very big tree full of new leaves, rooted on the summit of a little green hill, the spark of light shining brightly in your womb.

Breathing out, see yourself walking down the hill knowing you are the mother of this new egg that is soon to be fertilized.

©2005 Dr. Catherine Shainberg

Weaving your child's life tapestry and name
(Introduced in Chapter 8 with Janet and Leo)

Close your eyes. Breathe out slowly three times, counting from 3 to 1, seeing the numbers in your mind's eye. See the number 1 as tall, clear, and bright.

Imagine that you are sitting in front of your loom. In your lap, you have many skeins of colored wool.

Breathe out. Turn your eyes inward to contact your child. Ask him what color you should use. See the color that pops up for you, and start weaving.

Breathe out. Each time you change color, check with your child and see which color pops up.

Breathe out. When you feel that your tapestry is done, look at the scene you have woven.

Breathe out. If you feel something needs to be changed, do so. Do this until you are satisfied.

Breathe out. Turn your eyes inward and check with your child that the tapestry of his life is to his liking.

Breathe out. Ask his name. If you feel satisfied with it, weave it into the tapestry.

Breathe out. Open your eyes, seeing the tapestry with open eyes and hearing his name.

DreamBirth: Transforming the Journey of Childbirth through Imagery by Catherine Shainberg. Published by Sounds True, ©2014. All rights reserved. Exercise 46, page 98. http://www. SoundsTrue.com   Reprinted with permission of publisher.

Repotting the plant

(Introduced in Chapter 8 with Janet and Leo)

Close your eyes. Breathe out slowly three times, counting from 3 to 1, seeing the numbers in your mind's eye. See the number 1 as tall, clear, and bright.

See a potted plant in your home that isn't doing well.

Breathe out. Decide to break the pot in which it sits. Free the roots of the plant from the old soil.

Breathe out. Gather all the pieces of the old pot and the old soil into a black garbage bag. Take the garbage bag out and throw it into the garbage truck that is driving by.

Breathe out. You have prepared a bigger and more beautiful new pot for your plant. Fill it with fresh, rich, dark soil.

Breathe out. Plant your plant into the rich, new soil.

Breathe out. Take a pitcher of clear spring water and water your plant. Watch what happens.

Breathe out. Open your eyes.

DreamBirth: Transforming the Journey of Childbirth through Imagery by Catherine Shainberg. Published by Sounds True, ©2014. All rights reserved. Exercise 17, page 42. http://www. SoundsTrue.com   Reprinted with permission of publisher.

Clearing the office of the mind
(Introduced in Chapter 8 with Janet and Leo)

Close your eyes. Breathe out slowly three times, counting from 3 to 1, seeing the numbers in your mind's eye. See the number 1 as tall, clear, and bright.

Pay attention to a message that you received in childhood or during some relationship in your life, that you don't want to keep anymore, for example; 'you are bad', 'you are not lovable', 'you will never change'.

Breathe out. Go up to the office of your mind taking with you a big black garbage bag. Find all the files, books, tapes, videos that contain this message, and throw them into the black garbage bag.

Breathe out. Tighten the strings of your bag, throw it over your left shoulder and take it out of the office of your mind. Take it down and out of your house and crossing the road walk into the landscape. Take a shovel, a chisel and a hammer with you.

Breathe out. Dig a big hole, and throw the bag into the hole. Burn it. Watch it turn to ashes.

Breathe out. Cover the hole, asking mother earth to take care of the ashes. Find a big boulder and roll it over the covered hole. With the chisel and hammer chisel the opposite message, for example; 'I am loved', 'I am worthy', 'change comes easily.'

Once you chiseled the new message on the stone, return home knowing you have changed your destiny.

Breathe out, and open your eyes.

©2005 Dr. Catherine Shainberg

Changing the Past

(Introduced in Chapter 8 with Noemi and Mike)

Changing the Past has several parts to it: Reversing, Tikkun, Return, A New Past, New Present, and A New Future. All parts are done at the same time, one after the other. You can reverse on any emotion that is needed: fear and anxiety, anger and frustration, guilt and resentment, and so on.

Reversing on Fear and Anxiety

Breathe out slowly three times. Return back to the first time you felt fear and anxiety. How old are you? What was the event? Where is it located? Who are the people involved? Allow yourself to feel the pain as you felt it then. Do not shy away from it. Acknowledge your pain. You don't want to do it the injury of separating from it again. Feel it completely. Breathe out once. Move forward to the next event where you felt fear and anxiety. Do so for as many events as you can remember, at this time till you have surveyed all the events you can remember, at this time, where you felt fear and anxiety. Then move forward in time until you reach the present moment.

Kabbalah and the Power of Dreaming by Catherine Shainberg. Published by Inner Traditions International and Bear & Company, ©2005. All rights reserved. Page 153. http://www. Innertraditions.com   Reprinted with permission of publisher.

Tikkun Exercise

Breathe out three times. Imagine that you have a strong garden broom, the old kind made of branches. You also have a powerful garden hose and a knife, in case you need them. Return back through all the places you just visited in your last exercise. Sweep each place clear of the resonance of fear and anxiety; sweep it out to the left. If this doesn't work, (if you still feel enthralled), use your hose. If necessary, cut the resonance with your knife. If there are people involved you don't want in your life anymore, sweep them to the left too. Remember it all goes to the left. Do that till you reach the first memory of pain. Then, having swept its resonance out, return to be in your mother's womb. If that is not comfortable, see yourself bathing in God's clear waters on this Earth. You are His perfect child again. You can be born again, corrected, renewed, and perfected.

A New Past, New Present

Breathe out once. Imagine being born again perfect. See yourself journeying through all the places where the difficult events in your life, as you have identified them above, took place. But now they are free of the old resonance. The facts may be the same, but you are not ensnared by them anymore. You pass, unfettered, free, thus creating a new past. Pass through each place until you come to the new present. Live it fully.

A New Future

Breathe out once. See yourself in your new future. See yourself in a month's time. What do you look like? Where are you? Are you alone or with others? What are you doing? What is the feeling? Breathe out once. See yourself in three months' time. What do you look like now? Breathe out once. In a year's time; breathe out once. In five years' time. Breathe out once. Return to your new present, feel yourself in your new life, with your new past and your new future anchoring you firmly in the new present.

To call a soul that has passed

(Introduced in Chapter 8 with Noemi and Mike)

Close your eyes. Breathe out slowly three times, counting from 3 to 1, seeing the numbers in your mind's eye. See the number 1 as tall, clear, and bright.

See yourself on a vast plain at dusk looking toward the West and the setting sun. See the sea, the horizon, and the sky. Call out from the other side of the veil to the ancestor you wish to speak to. See that ancestor arriving across the ocean and the land to stand before you.

Breathe out. Tell that soul why you called It out to you. If you feel that something is incomplete between you, if you want to ask forgiveness, or you need clarification about something, do so now.

Breathe out. Listen to the response. Respond to what was said. Continue the conversation until you have reached a place of reconciliation or harmony. If necessary, ask, What do I need to do in this world, in this life, to make harmony and peace between us? If the answer is clear, and you both agree, then promise to do so.

Breathe out. Thank the soul for coming. Ask the soul to continue to speak to you through the dreamtime now that you have made this strong connection.

Breathe out. Say good-bye for now, knowing you will meet again. See the soul receding, over the land and ocean. Then continue watching until the soul disappears behind the veil.

Breathe out. Turn toward the east and watch the rising sun. Remember your promise to the soul knowing that you will manifest that promise in your life. Feel how the rising sun touches your body and gives you new energy and a lighter heart to go forward.

Breathe out, and open your eyes, feeling and seeing this with open eyes.

©2005 Dr. Catherine Shainberg

Reversing the past

(Introduced in Chapter 8 with Noemi and Mike)

Close your eyes. Breathe out slowly three times, counting from 3 to 1, seeing the numbers in your mind's eye. See the number 1 as tall, clear, and bright.

Tell your child that you are going to do an exercise now, that whatever emotions you feel should not concern her, and that all is well and she is safe in her amniotic sac, tucked under your heart.

Go back to the very first time you ever felt a difficulty with your mother. See where you are, what is happening, and how old you are.

Breathe out. Imagine that you, the adult, move to stand next to yourself as a child. Tell her you are protecting her now, and she can express what she feels to her mother. She must do so in the child's voice.

Breathe out. Tell her that you are going to cut the negative cord between her and her mother. Now cut the cord. What happens? If her mother fades away, you have cut the right cord. If not, know there is another invisible cord that needs to be cut. This time cut it with a sword. See her mother fading away.

Breathe out. Take the child out into a meadow to run and play. Play with her. Tell her she is now free to grow up.

Breathe out. See the child beginning to grow before your eyes through all the stages of childhood, adolescence, and young adulthood until you are both the same height and standing face to face.

Breathe out. Look into the eyes of this other you and embrace her. See and live what happens when you embrace.

Breathe out. Feel her merging into you, and be grateful that this lost part of you has returned to you.

Breathe out and open your eyes.

Speaking to another's Higher Self

(Introduced in Chapter 8 with Noemi and Mike)

Close your eyes. Breathe out slowly three times, counting from 3 to 1, seeing the numbers in your mind's eye. See the number 1 as tall, clear, and bright.

See that there are two chairs facing each other. See someone with whom you have had some difficulty come sit in one of the chairs. See yourself sitting in the other chair, facing that person. Get up and taking a chalk out of your pocket, draw an infinity sign around the two chairs. Draw it twice so that there's a path between the two infinity signs.

Now each of you is sitting in a different circle.

Breathe out. When the breath comes in through your nostrils, see the breath very blue, descending into your mouth. Blow it out into the pathway between the two infinity signs and see it running very fast in the path between the two circles.

Breathe out. Imagine that your chairs are propelled upward through the movement, until you both reach your higher selves. Tell the other person what you wish to say. Listen to the answer; respond until some kind of understanding or resolution is reached. As soon as this happens you will know it as your chairs return to the ground.

Breathe out. Imagine that you stretch your hand up into the heavens, and catch a sword of saphire blue light. Cut any negative cords between the two of you.

See the two circles separating and floating away, so that each one of you is now separate and strong in your own space.

Breathe out, open your eyes.

© 2005 Catherine Shainberg
(Adapted from Phyllis Krystal, *Cutting the Ties that Bind*)

The castle
(Introduced in Chapter 8 with Noemi and Mike)

Close your eyes. Breathe out slowly three times, counting from 3 to 1, seeing the numbers in your mind's eye. See the number 1 as tall, clear, and bright.

Imagine that you are part of an army that is trying to take over a fortified castle. You are a knight on horse or on foot rushing with the rest of the soldiers towards the big gates of the castle. Find a way to break into the fortified castle.

Breathe out. When you have gained access to the castle, grab a torch and run down the dungeon steps prying open the prison doors and letting the prisoners out.

Continue on down, until you come to the deepest dungeon. Break open the door and enter.

Who do you find? Help the person out of the prison cell and up the steps toward the light of day.

Breathe out. Now guide the freed person out of the fortified castle and into nature. Find a way to help this person to recover their health and sanity. When the person has recovered, embrace looking deep into their eyes and experience what happens.

Breathe out and open your eyes.

©2005 Dr. Catherine Shainberg

Looking at important males in your life
(Introduced in Chapter 8 with Mike and Noemi)
(This exercise can also be used for important females. Substitute the word 'female'/'woman' in all instances that the word 'male'/'man' is used.)

Close your eyes. Breathe out slowly three times, counting from 3 to 1, seeing the numbers in your mind's eye. See the number 1 as tall, clear, and bright.

Imagine looking into a mirror and seeing the face of the last man that you have had an important relationship with.

Look into the eyes of the man. Sweep off to the left out of the mirror what you haven't liked about him and now look at what he has given you that is good.

Thank him for what he has given you that is good, saying that you will cherish in your heart that particular quality or gift that was his.

Breathe out, and sweep his image to the left, if that person is no longer in your life, or to the right if that person is still in your life, but in a different relationship to you now.

Breathe out. Going backwards in time, see the next person. Continue on backward from male relationship to male relationship, always looking into the eyes of the one who appears, sweeping off to the left, out of the mirror what you haven't liked about him and asking to be shown clearly the gift he gave you. Thank him for the gift and let him go, sweeping him either to the left if that person is no longer in your life, or to the right if that person is still present in your life.

Continue doing this going backwards in time, until you come to closer relationships such as siblings, fathers, or grandfathers.

When you have gone through all of your male contacts in this way, breathe out and gather into your hands the many gifts you have been given. See how they become one dream object.

What is it that you hold in your hands now, and what do you feel when you see it? What do you do with it?

Breathe out and open your eyes.

©2005 Dr. Catherine Shainberg

The chalice
(Introduced in Chapter 8 with Lynn)

Close your eyes. Breathe out slowly three times, counting from 3 to 1, seeing the numbers in your mind's eye. See the number 1 as tall, clear, and bright.

Imagine that you are sitting under a tree on thick emerald- green grass.

Breathe out. See appearing in front of you a large golden chalice filled to the brim with precious stones of every color.

Breathe out. Watch as the sunlight touches the stones, brightening all the colors.

Breathe out. See the colors spreading to envelop you and your baby, creating a many-colored aura around both of you. Feel it soothing, healing, protecting you.

Breathe out. Open your eyes, seeing the aura with open eyes.

DreamBirth: Transforming the Journey of Childbirth through Imagery by Catherine Shainberg. Published by Sounds True, ©2014. All rights reserved. Exercise 36, page 79. http://www. SoundsTrue.com   Reprinted with permission of publisher.

Taking your mother out of your body

(Introduced in Chapter 8 with Lynn)

(This exercise can be used for anybody else: father, parent, grandparent, or ex that may be in your body!)

Close your eyes. Breathe out slowly three times, counting from 3 to 1, seeing the numbers in your mind's eye. See the number 1 as tall, clear and bright.

Tell your child that you are going to do an exercise now, that whatever emotions you feel should not concern her, that all is well and she is safe in her amniotic sac, tucked comfortably under your heart.

Turn your eyes inward and find where your mother is lodged in your body. Tell her that you are now an adult and that having her in your body is no longer appropriate. Politely ask her to leave.

Breathe out. If she won't, lift your hands up to the sun, stretching your arms until your hands are close to the sun. Feel them getting warm and turning to light. Bring your hands down into your body. Take your mother by the shoulders and take her out of your body. Place her to the right or to the left of you, as you see fit.

Breathe out. Pour cool clear spring water into those spaces vacated by your mother. Ask every cell in your body to return to its natural healthy alignment.

Breathe out and open your eyes, feeling free and whole.

DreamBirth: Transforming the Journey of Childbirth through Imagery by Catherine Shainberg. Published by Sounds True, ©2014. All rights reserved. Exercise 59, page 120. http://www. SoundsTrue.com   Reprinted with permission of publisher.

The tide

(Introduced in Chapter 8 with Lynn)

(This exercise is not to be done if you are pregnant. If you are not pregnant, it should only be done once every three months, never more frequently.)

Close your eyes. Breathe out slowly three times, counting from 3 to 1, seeing the numbers in your mind's eye. See the number 1 as tall, clear and bright.

Imagine you are at the ocean. Lie down in the sand with your feet at the edge of the waves.

Breathe out. Hear and sense a wave coming and touching the tips of your toes, entering your toes, and covering your feet. See and feel the salt water churning and turning inside your feet, and the salt water and sand scrubbing the skin of your feet. Feel this double massage scrubbing the inside and the outside of your feet vigorously.

Breathe out. Now the wave ebbs out of your feet through your toes, pulling the toxins out and into the depths of the ocean to be dissolved.

Look down at the inside of your feet, see that your feet are chambers of light, every muscle fiber is a fiber of light.

Breathe out. Hear another wave coming. It touches your toes, enters and covers all the way up to your hips; touches your fingers and goes up to your elbows, entering and covering your hands and forearms. See and feel that double massage, the sparkling, salty water washing, clearing, cleaning every part of the inside of your legs and forearms; the salt and sand scrubbing your skin on the outside.

Breathe out. And again, feel the wave receding, pulling out through the tips of your fingers and the tips of your toes all the toxins, all the memories, everything you no longer need that doesn't serve you, to be washed away into the depths of the ocean. Look down into your legs and arms seeing great chambers of light, every muscle fiber a fiber of light.

Breathe out. Hear another wave coming. It rushes in to touch your toes and fingers, enters and covers all the way up to your waist. See and feel that double massage of the inside of your pelvis, legs and forearms and of the outside with the salt and sand scrubbing your skin.

Breathe out. Feel the pull of the wave as it recedes out of your body through fingers and toes carrying away all old toxins and memories that have been dislodged by the massage. See the wave being pulled into the depths of the ocean. Look into your body and see the great chamber of light from your waist down, every muscle fiber taut and golden.

Breathe out. And again, a wave comes rushing in, a little louder and touches your toes and fingertips, enters and covers all the way up to the base of your neck. Feel the movement of the salt water going to every little corner and recess of the bones, in and out of every cavity, cleaning and clearing, dislodging old memories, old toxins you don't need. Sense the massage on the skin opening up your pores and cleansing your skin.

Breathe out. Feel the wave receding out of your body carrying all the toxins, all the old memories into the depths of the ocean to be dissolved by the salt.

Breathe out, and look into that great chamber of light stretching from your neck down to your feet. See every muscle taut and golden.

Breathe out. Hear a bigger wave come rushing in. It touches your toes, your fingertips, entering and covering you, all the way up to the base of your nose.

Feel as the salt water swirls around each of your vertebrae up to your cervical vertebrae, clearing them; the salt water and sand on the outside scrubbing your skin. Feel the salt water inside your mouth cleaning and clearing your teeth, your gums, your tongue, your vocal cords, while the skin is being scrubbed and cleansed on the outside.

Breathe out, and watch as the wave recedes dislodging whatever still needs to be washed away and dissolved.

Look down at this great chamber of light stretching from your palate all the way down to your feet. See all your muscle fibers taut and golden.

Breathe out and listen as the ocean goes quiet. Hear from your feet up all those golden fibers beginning to vibrate and sing. Propelled by the music, jump up, feeling light and refreshed. Catch a ray of sunlight, cocoon yourself in the light and walk away, feeling how buoyant and vibrant your body is.

Breathe out and open your eyes, seeing yourself cocooned in light.

©2005 Dr. Catherine Shainberg

The feather of truth
(Introduced in Chapter 9 with Amily)

Close your eyes. Breathe out slowly three times, counting from 3 to 1, seeing the numbers in your mind's eye. See the number 1 as tall, clear, and bright.

Look at Lady Justice. She holds golden scales in her left hand. See her placing the red feather of truth in one scale.

Breathe out. See yourself placing your question—see it as a dream object—in the other scale. If the scale dips, you know the answer is no. If the scales balance, the answer is yes.

Breathe out. Do not try to change or influence what you see. Accept and trust the answer that comes to you from inside yourself.

Breathe out. Open your eyes.

DreamBirth: Transforming the Journey of Childbirth through Imagery by Catherine Shainberg. Published by Sounds True, ©2014. All rights reserved. Exercise 66, page 131. http://www. SoundsTrue.com   Reprinted with permission of publisher.

Return to a place of love
(Introduced in Chapter 9 with Amily)

Close your eyes. Breathe out slowly three times, counting from 3 to 1, seeing the numbers in your mind's eye. See the number 1 as tall, clear, and bright.

Imagine retiring to your bedroom or to a place of harmony, like a garden or meadow, where you can feel quiet.

Breathe out. Return to the first time you fell in love with your current partner. See the moment and feel it. What color is the love in your heart?

Breathe out. Send this color as a bridge of light from your heart to your partner's heart. Whatever you want to say or show, send it over the bridge of light to your partner.

Breathe out. Listen and watch. You may receive a message in return.

Breathe out. Feeling more at peace, open your eyes.

DreamBirth: Transforming the Journey of Childbirth through Imagery by Catherine Shainberg. Published by Sounds True, ©2014. All rights reserved. Exercise 15, page 40. http://www. SoundsTrue.com   Reprinted with permission of publisher.

Stepping into someone else's shoes
(Introduced in Chapter 9 with Amily)

Close your eyes. Breathe out slowly three times, counting from 3 to 1, seeing the numbers in your mind's eye. See the number 1 as tall, clear, and bright.

Visualize that standing, facing you, a few feet away, is someone with whom you are currently having some difficulty.

Breathe out. Imagine yourself stepping out of your body, walking in your DreamBody over to that person, and going to stand in his or her shoes.

Breathe out. From this new vantage point, look back at yourself. How do you see yourself? What do you sense and feel?

Breathe out. What do you say to the "you" standing opposite? Say it, hearing yourself saying it in this person's voice.

Breathe out. Return back to your own body, and look back at the person you just left. What, if anything, has changed?

Breathe out. Open your eyes.

Take three steps back
(Introduced in Chapter 9 with Amily)

Close your eyes. Breathe out slowly three times, counting from 3 to 1, seeing the numbers in your mind's eye. See the number 1 as tall, clear, and bright.

Imagine that you take three steps back, sensing your movements. Breathe out. Now look at your partner—what do you feel?

(If there is no change either in the way you see your partner or in your feelings toward your partner, take three more steps back. You can do it three times if needed.)

Breathe out. Open your eyes.

DreamBirth: Transforming the Journey of Childbirth through Imagery by Catherine Shainberg. Published by Sounds True, ©2014. All rights reserved. Exercise 14, page 39. http://www. SoundsTrue.com   Reprinted with permission of publisher.

Blue vase

(Introduced in Chapter 10: Verification: Babies hear the exercises in the womb)

Find a quiet place where you are not likely to be disturbed and where you can relax. Sit in an armchair with your arms and legs uncrossed. Close your eyes.

Breathe out all that disturbs you, all that tires you, all that obscures you.

Breathe it out as a light smoke that is easily absorbed by the plant life around you.

When your breath comes in on the inhalation, see it blue and filled with sunlight like the radiant blue light from the sky.

See the blue gold light filling your nostrils, your mouth, your throat, and flowing down your back as a great river of light. See it filling your legs, your feet and your toes, and stretching out of your toes as long antennas of light.

See the light circulating up your legs to fill your pelvis.

See the clear blue light surrounding and cushioning the amniotic sac in which your baby is floating comfortably. See the light rising up into your chest, filling your breasts and radiating out of them.

See it flowing in and out of your heart until your heart becomes a glowing blue lamp.

See the light flow down your arms like smaller rivers of light, filling your hands and fingers, stretching out of your fingers as long antennae of light.

As you continue to breathe in the blue light, see the light continue to fill you.

See it begin to radiate out of the articulations of your joints, out of your ankles, knees, hips, shoulders, elbows and wrists.

See the light fill you until it radiates out of your skin in all directions. See yourself as a crystal vase filled with light, the light cushioning the globe of blue amniotic waters in which your baby floats. See yourself radiating light in all directions.

Breathe out, open your eyes, and see this with open eyes for a few seconds.

DreamBirth: Transforming the Journey of Childbirth through Imagery by Catherine Shainberg. Published by Sounds True, ©2014. All rights reserved. Exercise 47, page 100. http://www.SoundsTrue.com   Reprinted with permission of publisher.

The garden—to prepare for procedures
(Introduced in Chapter 11: Testing the Imagery: My Bout with Cancer)

Close your eyes. Breathe out slowly three times, counting from 3 to 1, seeing the numbers in your mind's eye. See the number 1 as tall, clear, and bright.

You are walking around the base of a circular wall. Above the wall, you see the tops of trees. Walk until you find the gate. The key is in the lock. Open the gate and walk into the garden.

Breathe out. What does your garden look like?

Breathe out. Walk deeper into the garden and find a patch of thick, soft, emerald-green grass next to a tree and a running brook.

Breathe out. Lie on the grass in the shade of the tree and listen to the sounds of the brook and the birds, feeling how your body rhythms become attuned to the rhythms of Nature.

Breathe out. Now invite those you trust to come into the garden, one by one, and to sit in a semi-circle around your head. Feel their love and attentiveness to you and to your unborn child.

Breathe out. When all of your witnesses have come in and sat down around you, and you feel comfortable and at ease, show your body in a precise visualization exactly what is going to happen and ask permission of your body to allow the procedure your doctor is about to perform.

Breathe out. If your body refuses permission, ask your body what it needs to accept the procedure. Respond to the needs of your body in images.

Breathe out. Once your body has given permission, ask permission of your baby to allow the procedure.

Breathe out. If your baby refuses permission, ask your baby what he needs to accept the procedure. Respond to the needs of your baby in images.

Breathe out. Invite your doctor, assistants, and nurses to come into the garden with their medications and tools. When they stand before you, see how the sunlight pours down onto their heads and into their arms and hands so that everything they touch— medications, tools, your body—turns to light.

Breathe out. See that all is done perfectly. Check with your baby that all is well.

Breathe out. See the doctor, assistants, and nurses leaving.

Breathe out. Feel all of your loved ones still around you, guarding and protecting you and your baby; feel their love and their joy. When you are ready, see them go one by one out of the garden. The gate closes after the last one, and you are alone with your baby.

Breathe out. Feel the rhythms of nature; feel your body and your baby breathing with the rhythms of nature.

Breathe out. When you are ready, get up and slowly walk out of your garden with your baby tucked safely under your heart (or held in your arms), close the gate, and take the key or put it in a place where you will always be able to find it.

Breathe out. Walk into your future confident and serene.

DreamBirth: Transforming the Journey of Childbirth through Imagery by Catherine Shainberg. Published by Sounds True, ©2014. All rights reserved. Exercise 156, page 287. http://www. SoundsTrue.com   Reprinted with permission of publisher.

Exchanging Parts with the Guardian Angel

(Introduced in Chapter 11: Testing the Imagery: My Bout with Cancer)

Close your eyes. Breathe out slowly three times, counting from 3 to 1. See the 1 tall, clear, and bright.

Stand in your meadow and look up into the blue sky. Let your eyes wander across the sky until you land on the deepest blue of the sky.

Breathe out. Let your eyes gaze into the deepest blue and call on your guardian angel to appear.

Breathe out. See your guardian angel in all the glorious light he is composed of.

Breathe out. Ask for permission to exchange your diseased parts with your guardian angel's parts.

Breathe out. See your diseased parts rising up to be transformed into light, your angel's parts of light descending to replace your body parts.

Breathe out. See your body filled with the goodness of your angel's light.

Breathe out. Open your eyes, seeing this with open eyes.

The Kabbalah of Light by Catherine Shainberg. Published by Inner Traditions International and Bear & Company, ©2022. All rights reserved. Exercise 137, pages 270–271. http://www.Innertraditions.com   Reprinted with permission of publisher.

Bibliography

Achterberg, Jeanne. *Imagery in Healing: Shamanism and Modern Medicine.* Boston: Shambhala, 1985.

_____, Barbara Dossey and Leslie Kolkmeir. *Rituals of Healing: Using Imagery For Health and Wellness.* New York: Bantam Books, 1994.

Aurand, Paul. *Essential Healing.* Oakland, CA: Reveal Press, 2021.

Benyosef, Simcha. *Reversing Cancer through Mental Imagery.* New York: ACMI Press, 2016.

Bodine, Echo. *What Happens When We Die: A Psychic's Exploration of Death, Heaven, and the Soul's Journey After Death.* Novato, CA: New World Library, 2013.

Bowman, Carol. *Children's Past Lives.* New York: Bantam Books, 1997.

Braden, Gregg. *Spontaneous Healing of Belief: Shattering the Paradigm of False Limits.* Carlsbad, CA: Hay House, 2008.

Chamberlain, David B. *Babies Remember Birth.* New York: Ballantine Books, 1988.

_____. *The Mind of Your Newborn Baby.* Berkley, CA: North Atlantic Books, 1998.

Carman, Elizabeth and Neil Carman. *Cosmic Cradle: Spiritual Dimension of Life Before Birth.* Berkeley, CA: North Atlantic Books, 2000, 2013.

Cooper, Diana. *Birthing a New Civilization: Transition to the New Golden Age In 2032.* Rochester, VT: Findhorn Press, 2009, 2011, 2013.

_____ and Tim Wheld. *The Archangel Guide to Enlightenment and Mastery.* Carlsbad, CA: Hay House, 2016.

Coudris, Manuel David. *Diary of an Unborn Child, An Unborn Baby Speaks From Its Mother's Womb*. Bath: Gateway Books, 1992.

Emoto, Masaru. *Messages from Water*. Japan: Hado Publishing, 2002.

_____. *Messages from Water and the Universe*. Carlsbad, CA: Hay House, Inc., 2010.

_____. *The Healing Power of Water*. Carlsbad, CA: Hay House, Inc., 2004.

_____. *The Hidden Messages in Water*. New York: Atria Books, 2001.

_____. *The True Power of Water*. New York: Atria Books, 2003.

Epstein, Gerald. *Healing Into Immortality: A New Spiritual Medicine of Healing Stories and Imagery*. New York: Bantam Books, 1994.

_____. *Healing Visualizations: Creating Health Through Imagery*. New York: Bantam Books, 1989.

_____. *The Encyclopedia of Mental Imagery: Colette Aboulker-Muscat, 2,100 Visualization Exercises for Personal Development, Healing, and Self-Knowledge*. New York: ACMI Press, 2012.

Gabriel, Michael. *Voices from the Womb*. Lower Lake, CA: Aslan Publishing, 1992.

Goldner, Diane. *A Call to Heal*. Santa Monica, CA: Golden Spirit Books, 2013.

_____. *How People Heal: Exploring the Scientific Basis for Subtle Energy in Healing*. Charlottesville, VA: Hampton Roads Publishing Company, 2003.

Hallet, Elisabeth. *Stories of the Unborn Soul*. New York. Writers Club Press, 2002.

Hart, Tobin. *The Secret Spiritual World of Children*. Maui, HI: Inner Ocean Publishing, 2003.

Hellinger, Bert. *Love's Hidden Symmetry*. Phoenix, Arizona: Zeig, Tucker & Co., 1998.

Hendrix, Harville and Helen LaKelly Hunt. *Getting the Love You Want: A Guide for Couples.* New York: St. Martin's Griffin, 1988, 2008, 2019.

Hunt, Valerie. *Infinite Mind: Science of the Human Vibrations of Consciousness.* Malibu, CA: Malibu Publishing Co., 1996.

Jones, Carl. *Mind Over Labor.* New York: Penguin Books, 1987.

Kern, Michael. *Wisdom in the Body: The CranioSacral Approach to Essential Health.* London: HarperCollins Publisher, 2001.

Kluny, Rita. *Your Baby Remembers.* 21st Century Baby Press, 2011.

Kryon Channelings, 1997–2023, Kryon.com, https://www.menus.kryon.com

Krystal, Phyllis. *Cutting the Ties that Bind: Growing Up and Moving On.* Red Wheel/Weiser, 1993, 2009.

Leibowitz, Judith and Bill Connington. *The Alexander Technique.* New York: Harper Perennial, 1991.

Lipton, Bruce. *The Biology of Belief: Unleashing the Power of Consciousness, Matter & Miracles.* Carlsbad, CA: Hay House, 2015.

Makichen, Walter. *Spirit Babies: How to Communicate with the Child You're Meant to Have.* New York: Bantam Dell, 2005.

Marks, Jeffrey. *The Afterlife Interviews, Volume 1.* Lynwood, WA: Arago Press, 2012.

McCarty, Wendy. *Welcoming Consciousness: Supporting Wholeness from the Beginning of Life. Santa Barbara*, CA. Wondrous Beginnings Publishing, 2012.

McManus, Mary Grace. *Cheyenne, Journey to Birth.* Lynwood, Washington: Clay Mountain Press, 1999.

Miller, Carolyn. *Creating Miracles: Understanding the Experience of Divine Intervention.* Tiburon, CA: H J Kramer, Inc., 1995.

Moss, Robert. *Conscious Dreaming.* New York: Crown Trade Paperbacks, 1996.

Muranyi, Monika and Kryon. *The Women of Lemuria: Ancient Wisdom for Modern Times*. Outremont, Canada: Ariane Books, 2018.

Nelson, Dr. Bradley. *The Emotion Code. Mesquite*, Nevada: Wellness Unmasked Publishing, 2007.

Newton, Michael. *Destiny of Souls*. Fort, Mumbai: Jaico Publishing House, 2020.

Park, Glen. *The Art of Changing: A New Approach to the Alexander Technique*. Bath, Great Britain: Ashgrove Press Limited, 1989.

Rinpiche, Sogyal. *The Tibetan Book of Living and Dying*. New York: Harper Collins, 1994.

Roberts, Jane. *The Nature of Personal Reality: A Seth Book*. New York, Bantam Press, 1978.

_____. *The Magical Approach: A Seth Book*. San Rafael, CA. Amber-Allen Publishing, 1995.

_____. *The Way Towards Health: A Seth Book*. San Rafael, CA: Amber-Allen Publishing, 1997.

Shainberg, Catherine. *DreamBirth: Transforming the Journey of Childbirth through Imagery*. Boulder, CO: Sounds True, Inc., 2014.

_____. *Kabbalah and the Power of Dreaming*. Rochester, VT: Inner Traditions, 2005.

_____. *The Kabbalah of Light*. Rochester, VT: Inner Traditions, 2022.

Shaloe, Alison. *Baby Talk to Me*. The Unbound Press, 2022.

Sills, Franklyn. *CranioSacral Biodynamics*. Berkeley, CA: North Atlantic Books, 2001.

Spangler, David. *Everyday Miracles: The inner art of manifestation*. Bantam Books, 1996.

Upledger, John E. *Your Inner Physician and You: CranioSacral Therapy and Somato Emotional Release*. Berkely, CA: North Atlantic Books, 1997.

Verny, Thomas and Pamela Weintraub. *Pre-Parenting, Nurturing Your Child from Conception*. New York: Simon and Schuster, 2002.

_____ and John Kelly. *The Secret Life of the Unborn Child*. New York: Dell Publishing, 1981.

Vitale, Joe and Ihaleakala Hew Len. *Zero Limits: The Secret Hawaiian System for Wealth, Health, Peace and More*. Hoboken, NJ: John Wiley and Sons, 2007.

Wagner, Ursula and Wilfried Fink. *Anima: Symbole des Erinnerns*. Edition Amo, 2006.

Weiss, Brian. *Many Lives, Many Masters*. New York: Simon and Schuster, 1992.

_____. *Messages from the Masters*. New York: Grand Central Publishing, 2000.

Wright, Machaelle Small. *Behaving as if the God in All Life Mattered*. Jeffersonton, VA: Perelandra, Ltd, 1987.

About the author

Claudia Rosenhouse Raiken's formal training consists of a Masters from NYU in Dance and Kinesiology; Dance Therapy training and certification with Blanche Evan, a pioneer in her field; Alexander Technique (trained and certified by Alan Katz); and CranioSacral Therapy (through the Upledger Institute and Biodynamic CranioSacral through the Wellness Institute). Since 1996, Raiken has been a practitioner of Alexander Technique, and since 2004, a CranioSacral therapist. Her training at the School of Images began in 2003. She became the catalyst, playing a crucial part in the development of *DreamBirth* Imagery, becoming a certified practitioner in 2010. She began giving private sessions through the school in 2010 and is a member of the faculty, currently teaching *DreamBirth* classes, and running their *DreamBirth* Certificate Program. Raiken is a certified Birth Doula and Childbirth Educator, and co-founder of The Birth Studio, where *DreamBirth* Imagery is the primary modality used. Imagery is now the main component of her work: as it has been integrated into her body-work practice and included in her work with conception and fertility, and through the School of Images.

During Raiken's Alexander Technique training however, that her real adventure and passion for Imagery began. A visiting professor came to one of her classes, suggesting a very specific and quick "image." Instantly her neck and back released, making her whole body free and easy, her spine deliciously long. Astonishing! One quick image become equivalent to months, or in some instances, years of work. A few months later, at a CranioSacral Workshop, her life changed. After watching her work, one of the assistants told her about The School of Images. And so, in 2003 Raiken asked Catherine Shainberg to teach her imagery for pregnancy and childbirth. Claudia was hooked. So not only did she participate in the weekly class with other birth professionals, but she began to take all classes given at the school, as well as a weekly private session with Catherine. Since 2003, she has been taking classes continuously at the school, including Supervision and Prayer, and has participated in every workshop Catherine has given in New York. In 2012 Claudia assisted Catherine when she presented *DreamBirth* to a group of obstetricians in Russia.

Two years into the work Raiken developed cancer of the uterine lining. The discipline she was teaching her clients suddenly became life or death for her, using imagery to help fight the cancer and to face the demons and underlying emotions that were emerging. The imagery alleviated the side effects of both chemotherapy and radiation. When Claudia beat the cancer, the very real benefits of the work became crystal clear, claiming that the experience with cancer gave her a PhD in Imagery. It jump-started her into the creative and revelatory aspects of the work, and to become a grateful recipient of the healing it promoted. As Catherine often says, "You plunged in—and the work took on a life of its own, showing you the way." The imagery still informs Raiken and is the ever-present presence in her life and work; amazing her daily with what it can do, and the richness it gives all who work with it.

About the painter

Claudia Grotzek, Painter, Pearl diver, Trainer and Mother in Munich www.
claudiagrotzek.de

I paint light-energetic pictures/paintings for the soul and for living spaces. My intention is to touch people's hearts with my pictures and to bring lightness and joy. Colors are my world. With my workshops I train people to tap into their creative power and inner knowledge.

As Claudia asked me for an image for the cover of *Messages from the Womb*, I was very excited. Claudia had accompanied me with *DreamBirth* during my pregnancy and I had the gift of bringing my daughter into the world with *DreamBirth* at home in Munich with her support. *DreamBirth* is so much more. I like to think back to the time when I did the exercises with my daughter in my womb and all the conversations I was allowed to have with her. Today, I can see the fruits of the seed planted back then with *DreamBirth*, creating a naturally strong and trusting bond with my daughter from the inside out.

The Iris flower Painting on the bookcover is a detail of the Iris Lilie. Capturing the essence of flowers, the blossoming within ourselves—the fullness and the feminine. The theme of the cover is a wonderful co-creation among all of us.

During my pregnancy with my daughter, I painted the ANIMA symbols—a collection of free symbols of clairvoyant children*. These symbols introduce each chapter of Messages from the Womb. The colors are inspired by my daughter, who told me to play with it as she grew within the womb. The ANIMA symbols speak a global language of the heart from a pure child's perspective. They are very simple and easy. I have taken this language, which radiates the lightness and joie de vivre of a child, and translated it into colorful art paintings. For more information and paintings please visit the website.

* Ursula Wagner and Wilfried Fink, *ANIMA: Symbole des Erinnerns*, 2006 Edition Amo, Book and set of cards (Ursula and Wilfried received these symbols from children after attending a workshop with James Twyman "Indigo Power" in 2005.)

PUBLICATIONS

Since IML's humble erratic beginnings, the mascot, which has reverently danced across our newsletter, the watermarks of the website, the original interiors, and now these front and back pages, is a graphic symbol of the Kalahari San Bushmen's Trickster God, the praying mantis, who has forever—or for as long as they can remember—been inspiring the mythological stories of these First People who nomadically walk the earth whenever they can, as our nomad authors write their way through life.

www.ingramcontent.com/pod-product-compliance
Lightning Source LLC
Chambersburg PA
CBHW061144120626
46546CB00005B/1917